C000265384

FERRARI DINO

Other Titles in the Crowood AutoClassics Series

FERRARI DINO

The Complete Story

Anthony Curtis

First published in 1990 by
The Crowood Press,
Ramsbury, Marlborough,
Wiltshire SN8 2HE

Paperback edition 1997

© The Crowood Press 1990

All rights reserved. No part of this publication may be reproduced
or transmitted in any form or by any means, electronic or
mechanical, including photocopy, recording, or any information
storage and retrieval system, without permission in writing from
the publishers.

British Library Cataloguing in Publication Data

A catalogue record for this book is available
from the British Library

ISBN 1 86126 065 2

Printed in Hong Kong by Paramount Printing Co. Ltd.

Contents

Acknowledgements

A number of people and organisations have been very helpful to me during the preparation of this book, but in particular I owe thanks to Ken Bradshaw, secretary of the Ferrari Owners' Club, Mark Konig of Maranello Concessionaires Ltd, Colin Clarke of Colin Clarke Engineering Ltd, Kevin O'Rourke of MotoTechnique Ltd, Bob Houghton of Bob Houghton Ltd, Robert Abraham and John Godfrey. Thanks are also due to Eric Branson for checking the factual accuracy of the manuscript, Reed Business Publishing for granting permission to reproduce numerous extracts from *Motor*, and to Doug Nye for personal assistance and for being the author of that invaluable source book on racing Dinos called *Dino – The Little Ferrari*.

Anthony Curtis, 1990

The photographs in this book were kindly supplied by the Motoring Picture Library, Beaulieu, with the following exceptions: page 28 (Quadrant Picture Library); and pages 56–7, 114 top, 118, 121, 123 top, and 124–5 (Mark Konig).

The line drawings on pages 23, 46, 47, 71, 72, 73, 102, 103, 107, 127, 128, 129, 140 and 158 were drawn by Terry Hunns; and those on pages 38, 39, 42, 43, 123 below left and right, 151, 154, and 162–3 are reproduced courtesy of Ferrari SEFAC SpA.

A Brief History of the Ferrari Dino

Evolution

October 1965	Pininfarina show Dino Berlinetta styling exercise at Paris Show. Has air scoops in flanks and rear buttress/glazing arrangement but otherwise different from final car with in-line engine.
November 1966	Pininfarina show Dino Berlinetta GT at Turin Show. Very similar to final car, but still with in-line engine.
November 1967	Pininfarina show Dino 206GT at Turin Show, with transverse engine giving luggage space. Same as production car in all but minor detail.

Production – 206GT

Mid-1968	Production of 206GT begins; chassis no. of first car believed to be 00104.
Summer 1969	206 production finishes, probably at chassis no. 00398; some 150 cars built, all left-hand drive. Five imported new to UK.

Production – 246GT and 246GTS

Type L or Series I
Chassis nos. 00400–01116; 357 cars

Autumn 1969	Start of 246 production; centrelock wheels retained.
Autumn 1970	End of Series I.

Type M or Series II
Chassis nos. 01118–02130; 507 cars

September 1970	Production of Series II begins following completion of Fiat-financed extension to Maranello factory. Bolt-on wheels introduced.
October 1970	First right-hand drive car available for UK.
July 1971	End of Series II.

Type E or Series III.
Chassis nos. 02130–08518; 3019 cars

August 1971	Start of Series III.
March 1972	Open GTS model with Targa roof introduced at Geneva Show.
Spring 1972	Dino with exhaust emission controls introduced to US market.
1974	Production of 246 Dino finishes; replacement with 308GT4.

The Ferrari Dino 246 must lay claim to being the most beautiful car ever produced.

1 Conception

To the newcomer, the world of classic cars must seem dauntingly complex. Long before broadened definitions brought a new image to the humble Morris Minor, dozens of cars were regarded as 'classic' for one reason or another, and since then the list has swelled by the numerous additional models of special distinction that have appeared during the post-war years. Many of these so-called classic cars, of course, owe their status to little more than their age, yet even when these are excluded there remains a substantial élite, genuinely superior to their contemporaries in appearance, performance or design − or some combination of all three.

This book, however, is about a car which lies above that élite in turn, one which lies in a class distinguished by a still higher level of excellence and charisma, a class composed of no more than a handful of cars altogether. It is about the Ferrari Dino 246.

Sceptics will immediately want to know what can possibly be so wonderful about one particular design out of all the thousands that have been created in the century-long history of the motor vehicle. The question is not easily answered because we're in an area of hype and hyperbole, of fantasy and flamboyance, where poetry all too easily teeters over into pretension.

Briefly, though, there are four basic reasons why the Ferrari Dino 246 is widely acknowledged as something very special indeed. It is beautiful to look at. It is very fast. It has particularly responsive and forgiving handling. It is the product of one of the world's finest and most highly respected manufacturers of sporting high-performance cars.

Unlike some other highly acclaimed classics, moreover, the Ferrari Dino has no serious weaknesses in areas of major importance − though its heating and ventilation system would certainly win no prizes. This apart, it is a car with a string of solid, no-nonsense, down-to-earth virtues which will be thoroughly explored as this narrative proceeds.

The subject of our attention is a two-seater high-performance sports car of the sort known as 'mid-engined'. The significance of this designation will later be considered in more depth, but for the moment it's sufficient to know that it refers to a car in which the engine lies behind the driver and passenger yet ahead of the rear wheels. For the Dino that engine is a transversely orientated watercooled V6 with four overhead camshafts which drives the rear wheels through a gearbox and final drive unit mounted beneath and behind it. In keeping with the racing heritage, all four wheels are located by double-wishbone independent suspension linkages and are braked by generously proportioned ventilated discs. The car is available in both closed and open versions, and has an extravagantly curved body notable for several unusual features.

The road-going Ferrari Dino first appeared in 1967 as the Ferrari Dino 206GT, when its bodywork was made of light alloy, as was its V6 engine, a 2-litre unit developing 180bhp at 8,000rpm. No more than about 150 of these were built however, and in 1969 a new, slightly larger, version of the car appeared, the 246GT, with a steel body and a bigger iron-block version of the engine with a capacity of 2,418cc and an output of 195bhp at 7,600rpm. It gave the car a maximum speed close to 150mph (241kph) and a 0−60mph acceleration time of around seven seconds – still fast by any standards. An open model, the 246GTS (S for Spider) was introduced in 1972, and by the time production ceased in 1974 nearly 4,000 246 Dinos of both types had been built, a tiny number by volume production standards but a very large one for a small company like Ferrari.

The few journalists lucky enough to drive those early 206 cars were highly enthusiastic about it, while the larger number able to test the 246 were lavish in their praise. Despite this favourable reception, though, Ferrari themselves seemed to have a rather ambiguous attitude towards the car. To begin with they deliberately distanced themselves a little from it, being careful not to call it a Ferrari but instead a Dino, in memory of Enzo Ferrari's son Alfredo or Alfredino who died at the age of twenty-four. In the early brochures the car was described as 'tiny, brilliant ... *almost* a Ferrari' (author's italics).

Such hesitancy was surprising in an organisation not noted for its humility. But the paradox it represents is only one of the several elements which together make up the complex and fascinating heredity of the road-going Dino. To understand it, we need first to examine the ultimate creator of the car, Enzo Ferrari, and the tradition he forged.

FERRARI – MAN AND MARQUE

In all the history of the motorcar, only three men have so far achieved legendary eminence as makers both of outstanding high-performance road cars and of consistently successful racing cars. Those three men are Ettore Bugatti (1881–1947), Enzo Ferrari (1898–1988) and Colin Chapman (1928–1982) of Lotus. Bugatti and Lotus enthusiasts will no doubt disagree, but nevertheless a powerful objective argument could be advanced to support the view that

The father of the marque: Enzo Ferrari, 'Il Commendatore'.

the Ferrari name can claim the greatest magic.

Consider the record. Apart from the Dino itself, almost every Ferrari model is now regarded as a classic, but those of special merit include the 750 Monza (1954–1955), the 410 Superamerica (1955–1959), the 250 Lusso (1962–1964), the 275 GTB and GTB4 (1964–1968), the 365GTB4 or Daytona (1968–1973) and the Berlinetta Boxer (1973–1981). The tradition continues today with the Testarossa and F40 models.

On the track the score is even more impressive. At the time of Enzo Ferrari's death in August 1988, the successes of his cars in Formula 1 racing included the winning of ninety-seven Grands Prix, ten Constructors' Cup titles, and nine Drivers' Championships. In sportscar racing the record included nine outright wins at Le

Mans, eight Mille Miglia wins, seven Targa Florio wins and numerous lesser victories.

The man responsible for these achievements was born in Modena, Italy, on 18 February 1898, the second son of Alfredo Ferrari who owned a small workshop making components for the railway industry. Like all children Enzo Ferrari entertained various ambitions, but the general direction of his life began to be determined in 1908 when he saw Felice Nazzaro win the Coppa Florio road race in a Fiat. He soon decided that he, too, would be a racing driver.

First, though, came an undistinguished school career, after which Enzo worked briefly in the family business. But his father died of illness in 1916, his brother Alfredo died shortly afterwards, and Enzo himself became seriously ill after being conscripted into the Italian army in 1917, struck down by the influenza epidemic of that year.

At the end of the Great War, though weakened by two operations, Ferrari began to look for work. Now thoroughly fascinated by cars and motor racing, he started to scratch a living delivering chassis. But he soon graduated from the road to the track and from 1919 onwards embarked upon a career as a racing driver, mostly for Alfa Romeo, with some success. 1924 was a particularly good year with wins at Savio, Polesine and Pescara in the inaugural Coppa Acerbo. For this victory the government made him a *Cavaliere dell'Ordine della Corona d'Italia,* later raised to *Commendatore.* Although all such titles were declared null and void at the end of the war, many writers continued to describe Ferrari as *Commendatore.* He himself, however, never sought this, preferring to be called plain Ferrari or perhaps 'Ingegnere' (Engineer).

Despite this state recognition he had by then realised that he was a competent rather than inspired driver, though he continued to race intermittently until 1931. So he began to turn his attention away from the circuits by exploiting the wide range of contacts he

had built up in the bars of Turin and Milan amongst the engineers and test drivers of these highly industrialised areas in which Italy's motor industry was rapidly growing. He soon became known as a thrusting 'Mr Fixit' who made things happen and was entrusted with various tasks for Alfa Romeo on a semi-official basis, one of them being the poaching of senior engineering staff from Fiat, for Alfa's racing team. These activities were curtailed by Alfa Romeo's withdrawal from racing in 1925, yet he continued to work for the company in various ways particularly with a deep involvement in sales.

When Alfa Romeo returned to racing in 1929, he set up the Scuderia Ferrari with a number of shareholders and this organisation soon became Alfa's independent but official racing team. The association led to a string of Grand Prix successes in the early thirties, but from 1936 onwards Mercedes and Auto Union dominated the racing scene, and in 1938 the Scuderia Ferrari was taken over by Alfa Romeo. Ferrari was retained as director on a consultative basis, but disliked the big-company disciplines and lack of freedom to make decisions. He left, but retained both some capital and his own premises in Modena and after setting up a machine shop and getting some sub-contracting work, was soon back in racing with a pair of 1,500cc sports-racing cars based on Fiat components and called simply '815s' in accordance with his severance contract with Alfa Romeo which precluded the use of his name for four years.

These cars raced in 1940 but without success and the onset of the Second World War forced Ferrari to find other work. He became a manufacturer of machines that make ball bearings and achieved considerable success, weathering a move from Modena to the nearby village of Maranello dictated by government zoning plans, followed by a couple of allied bombing raids.

But Ferrari was impatient to return to

racing, and as soon as some measure of stability returned to Italy after the war he commissioned the distinguished engineer, Gioacchino Colombo to design a racing engine for him. With Colombo's agreement, Ferrari chose the V12 layout for his new power unit, influenced, it is said by the 1925 Formula 1 V12 Delage, and by the smoothness and flexibility of the V12 Packards he had driven. Colombo's V12 powered the first cars to bear the Ferrari name: the 125GP single-seater designed to compete in the 1.5-litre supercharged category of the immediate post-war Grand Prix formula, and the 125C sports-racer which was fitted with an unsupercharged version of the same engine. From then on, even though power units of many other types were to be produced over the years, the V12 engine became something of a Ferrari trademark. For decades Ferrari were the only post-war manufacturer in the world to sell road cars powered with V12 engines — until Jaguar introduced their own engine of the same kind in 1972.

But although Ferrari achieved some success on the circuits with these early V12s, and with some bigger engines of the same sort (designed by another well-known engineer, Aurelio Lampredi) his first major triumphs came in 1952 and 1953 with a four-cylinder car, the 500F2 with which both the drivers' and the constructors' championships were won.

Then followed a lean period brought on by the return of Mercedes to Formula 1 racing, but when the German company withdrew in 1955, Ferrari again became successful, firstly with a car taken over from Lancia, the Ferrari–Lancia D50 and then in 1958 with the Dino 246, a development of the first car to be named after Ferrari's son, a Formula 2 racer introduced in 1957.

Ferrari's reluctance to accept the changeover from front-engined to mid-engined cars in racing, which had been brought about by Cooper, was the cause of another lean period in Formula 1 until Phil Hill won the 1961

The great Mike Hawthorn, who drove Ferrari racing cars in the fifties, winning the Drivers' Championship with them in 1958.

Drivers' Championship in the (mid-engined) Dino 156. Then, in 1964, John Surtees won both Drivers' and Constructors' Championships in the 158, also mid-engined. The team's fortunes faded again for some years but surged back once more with a string of successes in the late seventies and early eighties. Today, Ferrari remains a major force in Grand Prix racing.

Until the late sixties, Ferrari's achievements in sportscar racing roughly followed the cycles of success and failure in Grand Prix racing. But since then they have been denied supremacy in this field by Ford's run of wins at Le Mans with the GT40s and their derivatives starting in 1967, and by Porsche's ensuing domination of the event (and others in the sportscar series) with the

917, while more recently both Jaguar and Mercedes have returned to claim wins.

In the first years of its existence, just after the Second World War, Ferrari followed practices traditional for a competition orientated company by selling a few replicas of their team cars for private entrants to race. Occasionally, a private owner would convert one of these for road use; it was in any case an era during which sports-racers could be driven on ordinary roads and Grand Prix cars could be given two-seater bodies when they had outlived their usefulness on the circuits.

By 1948, though, Ferrari had gone so far as to exhibit a pair of cars capable of road use at the Turin Motor Show, the open 166MM (Mille Miglia) and the closed 166 Inter Coupe. Some eighty of these were sold, all as rolling chassis upon which independent coach-builders constructed their own bodies.

The production and sale of bare chassis to be fitted with coachbuilt bodywork increased slowly, so that it was not until 1957 that the company made more than 100 cars in a year. Gradually, though, the company built up an association with the stylist Pininfarina and with the small coachbuilding company Scaglietti. Even so the numbers of road cars produced continued to remain very small for many more years.

Helped by an injection of capital from Fiat – who bought fifty per cent of the company's equity in 1969 – the production rate began to increase, but still slowly. Only in 1971, when manufacture of the 246 Dino got into full swing, did Ferrari's annual output exceed 1,000 cars, the total for that year being 1,246. Today, some 4,000 cars leave the factory every year, a puny number compared to the millions of cars manufactured annually by such giants as Fiat and Volkswagen, but quite large for a specialist constructor.

The company that Ferrari created is still prominent in Grand Prix racing and still makes some of the world's most exciting road cars. It is the formidable legacy of a formidable man who lived and breathed motor racing and participated in it with fanatical determination: to Enzo Ferrari nothing else mattered very much. He seldom bothered to conceal, for example, his view that the main reason for building road cars was to advertise his racing successes and to subsidise his racing activities. Because only the best would do for Ferrari, he hired the most talented engineers in Italy to design his racing cars; Gioacchino Colombo and Aurelio Lampredi were two such men, Vittorio Jano another.

But force is of little value without direction, and Ferrari complemented his unswerving will to succeed with a number of other valuable qualities. These included a sound and far-sighted judgement of both people and engineering trends. In asking Colombo to design a V12 engine for his first cars, for instance, he was choosing a configuration with inherent and fundamental advantages which are still valid today.

More specifically, Ferrari was convinced for most of his life that engine power was the key to the winning of races, stating in his own memoirs* his 'conviction that it is engine power which is – not 50 per cent but 80 per cent – responsible for succes on the track.' This proved to be one of the few of his beliefs which was not always correct: on a number of occasions his racers were beaten by less powerful but better handling rivals, and on a number of occasions he himself created cars which achieved success by combining good handling with adequate power. The original single-seater Dino and its eventual road-going successor were both cars of this kind.

DINO FERRARI

During the early part of his career as a racing driver, Ferrari met Laura, a pretty, smartly dressed girl from the village of Racconigi, a

* *The Enzo Ferrari Memoirs: My Terrible Joys;* Hamish Hamilton

village some twenty miles from Modena. With his uncertain future, Enzo must have seemed a poor prospect as a husband. Despite parental opposition, though, they quickly married — Ferrari does not disclose the exact date in his memoirs, merely saying that it was about 1920.

Like many men of powerful will and strong feelings, Ferrari craved a son, but it was not until some twelve years of marriage had elapsed that Laura gave him one — on 19 January 1932. He was christened Alfredo, but this was soon transformed into the affectionate diminutive Alfredino, or just Dino, for short.

After a typical childhood Dino Ferrari grew up into a young man with a great enthusiasm for motor racing and a keen interest in his father's activities. Enzo, in return, lavished pride and affection on him with all the intensity of his passionate nature, and began grooming him as his successor from an early age. Dino studied for an engineering diploma at the local Corni Institute and was enrolled by his father in a commerce course at the nearby University of Bologna as the first step towards gaining the wider experience necessary for managing the business, now an enterprise of considerable size and complexity.

As might be expected, Dino was given a succession of cars as soon as he was old enough to drive: first a Fiat 'Topolino' 500, then a Fiat 1100TV and after that a 2-litre Ferrari which he occasionally took to the Modena Autodrome racing circuit where his father recorded him as driving it 'fast and well'. But already the pride was tinged with anxiety, for Dino's health was poor. Of his enthusiasm for fast driving his father wrote 'This passion of his was a cause of concern to me, not so much for any risks that he might run, but because his health was precarious and I was afraid he might overtax himself'.

Enzo's fears proved to be well founded, because from the age of about twenty onwards Dino began to experience a slow, steady decline in health which was eventually diagnosed as muscular dystrophy. But he was a cheerful, courageous person, desperate to be a worthy successor to Enzo, and he fought hard against his disabilities. All who knew him — drivers like Phil Hill and Nino Farina, engineers like Vittorio Jano and Pino Allievi — have testified to his agreeable personality and sociable attitude.

Inevitably, though, attendances both at the university and at the Maranello factory became irregular. Dino's answer to the first problem was to enroll in an engineering correspondence course offered by the University of Fribourg, Switzerland. The course involved a thesis and he took as his subject the design of a 1.5-litre four-cylinder engine with three-valve combustion chambers. The second problem was partially resolved by the visits that Enzo, Jano and others paid him every evening to discuss their day's work.

Dino's illness made him vulnerable to infections that a healthy person might shrug off. In the winter of 1955 he was struck down by just such an infection, a nephritis virus that attacked his kidneys. His condition deteriorated still further and after a long struggle he died on 30 June 1956. At that time the treatment involved careful control of diet, and in his memoirs Enzo Ferrari writes touchingly about the final stages of his son's life:

'I had deluded myself — a father always deludes himself — that we should be able to restore him to health. I was convinced that he was like one of my cars, one of my motors; and I had thus drawn up a table showing the calories of all the foodstuffs he could eat without detrimental effect on his kidneys and, so that I might keep watch on the trend of his illness, I daily brought up to date a graph indicating the degree of albuminuria, the urinary specific gravity, the degree of azotemia, the diuresis and so on. Until one evening, in the notebook in which I put down all these particulars, I simply wrote "the match is lost" and, shutting the book said, "I have lost my son."'

Devastated, Ferrari was haunted by this loss for decades afterwards. For years he visited Dino's grave almost every day; and Dino's car was kept under a dust cover in a corner of the Modena servicing facility, exactly where Dino had parked it for the last time.

During that final winter, though, Dino had been able to make a bedside contribution to a lively debate on a topic that had been exercising the minds of the top engineering staff. This was to decide the best layout for the 1.5-litre unsupercharged engine that they intended to create for the new Formula 2 class of 1957. The possibilities considered included an in-line four-cylinder engine, a straight-six engine, a V6 unit or a V8 unit.

According to Enzo, his son Dino concluded that a V6 would be the best choice and Vittorio Jano 'accepted this decision'. Since Jano was an extremely gifted engineer of vast experience who needed advice from no-one, it may be suspected that he happened to share Dino's view and acquiesced in this version of events out of respect for Enzo Ferrari's grief and pride in his son.

Nevertheless, the V6 'Dino' engine which Jano went on to design as a result of these discussions was undoubtedly a fitting memorial to Enzo's brave and talented son.

THE ENGINE

In those debates at Dino Ferrari's bedside about the nature of the new Formula 2 engine for 1957, the talks would have been ruled by a number of fundamental engine design factors known to every good engineer.

The mid-engined layout of the tiny Cooper racing cars of the fifties inspired a similar, and equally successful, arrangement in the Ferrari Dino.

The highly successful 206S sports-racing car was powered by the same 65deg Dino V6 engine as the production model.

Perhaps the most important of these is piston area: other things being equal (though they seldom are) the greater an engine's piston area, the bigger its valves can be, the more fuel and air it can inhale in a given time and so the more power it can develop, *provided that it can be run fast enough to take advantage of the improved breathing ability without destroying itself.*

One way of realising a generous piston area is simply to endow an engine with a modest number of cylinders – say four – and to achieve the desired capacity by making the cylinders or bores very large in diameter and the stroke very short. Such an engine is described as being very 'oversquare' or to have a small 'stroke/bore ratio'. But this approach can only be carried so far, and a more profitable design philosophy is to adopt relatively conservative oversquare dimensions and then to take advantage of an odd quirk of geometry: if cylinder numbers are multiplied without increasing total capacity or altering the stroke/bore ratio, the stroke gets progressively shorter and the piston area progressively larger. Frictional losses,

Ferrari in close up

An insistence on the best possible engines and best possible drivers for his cars was only one of the more public and obvious aspects of Enzo Ferrari's ingrained ruthlessness. All his life he devoted much time to a ceaseless behind-the-scenes lobbying on behalf of his racing efforts. Using experience in publicity and journalism gained in his earlier years, he would tip off reporters, discreetly influence committees and play off one personality against another to win some advantage. He was legendary for the way in which he would needle drivers into greater efforts by leaking criticism of them through tame commentators. Sometimes this was not always to Ferrari's credit, his criticism of the great Juan Manuel Fangio being a particular example.

Enzo Ferrari could be arrogant and dictatorial, too. He always made it clear that he was the boss and it was solely he who made the decisions that mattered. Sometimes, though, when he seemed to be at his most despotic he quickly proved to be at his most far-sighted. When a major group of senior engineers and managers walked out in the early sixties thinking that Ferrari would be forced to ask them back, he dismissed them all, appointing in their stead younger men, among them the talented young engineer Mauro Forghieri, whom he had quietly been grooming for a senior post. The company went on — if anything profiting from the change.

But Ferrari was a complex, highly intelligent man, and a well-read one, in spite of being largely self-educated. There was a jocular and a kindly side to him as well as a ruthless one. He commanded so much respect that it was every racing driver's dream to be asked to join his team. Despite the political problems they knew they might face, they treated an invitation from Ferrari like a summons to an audience with the Pope.

It was also no secret that Ferrari liked women and women liked him, and that this mutual liking led to a number of affairs. The product of one of these was a son, Piero Lardi-Ferrari, who is now a senior executive of the company.

however, and the cost of construction, also rise as cylinder numbers are increased, putting a limit on the practical maximum.

But various other constraints would in any case have dissuaded Ferrari from adopting a highly complex design for their projected 1957 Formula 2 engine. Such an engine, like the V12 units they were already accustomed to building, would be too expensive for what was essentially to be a 'junior' racing formula. Even the V8 layout tentatively considered would have been at the upper limit of cost and suitability. The trick was to have just enough cylinders to achieve adequate superiority. Since Lotus and Cooper were planning to use the four-cylinder Coventry Climax engine, the decision made by Dino Ferrari and Vittorio Jano seems to have been just right.

Having decided the number of cylinders, the next step would have been to choose the best layout. In theory, again, the best layout might be regarded as the one giving the smoothest running, since although driver comfort is not of paramount importance in a single-seater, an engine that runs roughly generates nasty vibrations harmful not just to itself but also to the rest of the car. And smooth running in turn requires firing impulses that occur at regular angular intervals of crankshaft rotation and a cylinder layout which allows the acceleration forces on the reciprocating pistons and other parts to be fully balanced out.

With even firing intervals and perfect balance a straight six meets all these requirements – which is why it is so admirable a configuration for a road car. For competition, though, the considerable overall length of an in-line six not only makes it a big, bulky lump for a racing car, but also gives it a long crankshaft which is prone to torsional vibration at high rpm. By comparison a V6 engine is inherently much more compact, has imperfect but adequate balance and a short crankshaft easily made stiff enough to withstand very high revs. Once more the Ferrari decision is seen to have been a good one – a brave one, too, since although V6 engines are common on both road and track today, they were most unusual in the late fifties.

The next factor to consider would have been the valvegear which presents a further opportunity to improve an engine's breathing capacity. One obvious route to this improvement is to fit more than two valves; a pair of inlet valves and a single exhaust valve, perhaps, but more usually two inlet valves and two exhaust valves. This is because the total area of the *four* largest valves that can just be squeezed into a surface of given size is considerably greater than the *two* largest valves that can be squeezed in.

But although four-valve combustion chambers had been used in racing before, and although Dino was designing a three-valve cylinderhead for his correspondence course, even the Formula 1 Ferrari engines at that time had no more than two valves per cylinder. Any more than two, therefore, would not have been regarded as appropriate for the Formula 2 engine. But it would have been regarded as essential that those valves should open and close as positively as possible, and this could only be done by providing one camshaft for the inlet valves and another for the exhaust valves to eliminate the unwanted elasticity in the system that would have been introduced by rockers.

Four overhead camshafts, however, are not easy to accommodate on a V6 engine if one of the favoured angles between the banks of cylinders – 60 degrees – is used. The two upper camshafts tend to get in the way of the carburetters and inlet pipes that need to nestle in the vee. It was a problem to which Vittorio Jano gave considerable thought when he started to design the new V6 during the last weeks of Dino Ferrari's life. His solution was to open up the vee just a little, from 60deg to 65deg – enough to create more useful space but not so much as to have a major adverse effect on the balance condition.

This immediately created a difficulty: how to maintain firing impulses at the regular intervals of 120deg of crankshaft rotation inherent in a six-cylinder engine. (A single-cylinder four-stroke engine delivers one firing impulse every two revs or 720 degrees, so when there are six cylinders the combustion strokes should occur at 720/6 = 120deg of crankshaft movement.) Jano solved the problem by disposing the crankpins at either 55deg or 185deg intervals. (55deg + 65deg of bank angle = 120deg; 185deg−65deg of bank angle = 120deg.) The stroke and bore dimensions were fixed at 64.5mm×70mm giving a capacity of 1,489cc.

With all the fundamentals thus determined, Jano set to work on the details of the design. As had already become standard practice in V-engine design, the two banks of cylinders were staggered slightly, the left-hand bank being a little forward of the right, to accommodate side-by-side connecting rods (in place of the weaker fork-and-blade arrangement). These two banks were integrated with the crankcase into a single and very rigid light alloy casting into which cast iron cylinder liners were inserted. The water and oil pumps were driven off the nose of the crankshaft, as was a system of chains and tensioners driving the four overhead camshafts which acted on the valves through mushroom-type tappets screwed on to the valve stems. The engine breathed through three 38DCN Weber carburetters and dry-sump lubrication was adopted.

The valves were set at an included angle of 60deg in hemispherical combustion chambers featuring twin sparking plugs. These were fed from a pair of magnetos driven off the ends of the inlet camshafts and were so bulky that they added significantly to the overall length of the engine, partially negating its inherent compactness.

This, then, was the engine that burst into life some five months after Dino Ferrari's death, and which his father named after him, along with the Formula 2 car it was to propel. The new power unit was soon producing a claimed 180bhp at 9,000rpm compared to the 140bhp of the rival Coventry Climax engine, and was quickly fitted to the chassis built for it. The first outing of the car was on 28 April 1957 in a mixed Formula 1 and Formula 2 race at Naples where it was driven by Luigi Musso into third place against teammates Peter Collins and Mike Hawthorn driving the more powerful Formula 1 Ferraris of the day.

Thus began the racing career of the first car to be given the name 'Dino' by Enzo Ferrari. It soon proved so powerful and wieldy, that after a capacity increase to 2 litres it began to rival the lap times of the full-blown Formula 1 Ferraris. With a further increase in engine capacity to 2.4 litres, the car was upgraded to Grand Prix status and became the 246 Dino with which Mike Hawthorn won the 1958 Drivers' Championship for Ferrari. In 2-litre and 3-litre forms, the same 65deg Dino V6 engine also powered the successful 206S and 296S sports-racing cars.

For the next few years a succession of racing Ferraris bearing the Dino name appeared on the circuits of the world, though not all were powered by the 65deg V6 engine which is the concern of this book; in the early sixties Ferrari also built 60deg and 120deg V6 racing engines.

That original engine then faded from the scene somewhat until 1965 when, updated and redesigned by engineer Franco Rocchi it reappeared in the 166SP sports-racer. It was soon made clear that the same updated engine was once again destined for Formula 2, this time for the new 1.5-litre formula which was to start in 1967. There was a snag, though: the new regulations required that engines be 'production-based' and that at least 500 of them must have been built. At that time Ferrari's total annual production of road cars hardly reached 500 − it was 665 in 1966 − so he turned to Fiat for help. Fiat's Giovanni Agnelli agreed to help manufacture a 2-litre road-going version of the new Formula 2 engine in the minimum quantities required, and to provide a car, the Fiat Dino, to put those engines in. For Enzo, the arrangement provided an opportunity to increase profitability by creating around the same race-bred engine a new model, less powerful and less expensive than his mainstream products, but designed to sell in considerably larger numbers. The result of

A selection of pre-Dino Ferraris designed by Pininfarina. The 330GT (1964) above; 275GTS (1965) above right; and the 500 Superfast (1965) below right.

this thinking was, of course, a supposedly 'junior' Ferrari, the Dino.

THE MARKETPLACE

The decision to build a 'small' road-going Ferrari around the redesigned V6 Dino engine had roots that extended back many years. Several factors were involved, but most of all the fundamental problem that seems to have beset every company that has ever made prestigious high-performance cars in very small numbers.

The problem is easily stated: in this field of endeavour it is difficult to make money and easy to go broke. The basic cause of this sad state of affairs is that small manufacturers are seldom able to charge enough for a reasonable return on cars which are built largely by hand without significant economies of scale. Such companies are quickly put out of business, like Bentley and Bugatti, by recession or other setbacks; or else, like Aston Martin, have a history of continually changing ownership and financial crisis. And Ferrari laboured under an additional burden imposed by the high cost of financing their racing activities in the days before big-money sponsors took an interest in the Grand Prix scene.

A common response to this situation is to create what marketing men call an 'entry-level model', a relatively small, inexpensive car that will make the products of the company available to a wider range of people. Unfortunately, if the high standards of crafts-manship and design that give the marque its appeal are applied to the junior model, it tends to cost almost as much to make as its seniors, and thus is often sold at a loss, since it is essential that its price be kept down.

Nevertheless Ferrari began to explore this route in the late fifties by experimenting with a small-capacity four-cylinder engine, effectively built up from two-thirds of one bank of the current 250 V12 power unit. In 1959 a 950cc version of this engine developing 80bhp was fitted to a modified Fiat 1100 chassis and given a Fiat-style body by Pininfarina. The car was known to the press at the time as the 'Ferrarina' or sometimes in the works as 'The Tommy-gun' because the emblem devised for its radiator resembled the weapon of that name. Ferrari himself used this car for his personal transport, and it was also used for towing the Grand Prix cars.

At the 1961 Turin Show the project was seen to have advanced one stage further when Bertone displayed an elegant coupe, called simply the 'Mille', that was based on a Ferrari chassis and powered by a 1,032cc version of the four-cylinder engine. A Milanese industrialist acquired the rights to build the car, set up a company called ASA to do so, and at the Turin Show of the following year exhibited a car similar to the Bertone prototype called the ASA 1000GT. But deliveries did not begin until the end of 1964, some two years later, and the enterprise was a commercial disaster and ceased trading in 1967.

Denied the prosperity that royalty payments might have brought him, it's clear that Ferrari began to experience steadily increasing financial difficulties as the sixties rolled on. At the beginning of the decade he even considered a take-over by Ford, but withdrew at the last minute. After that came the collaboration with Fiat to produce the Dino engine in sufficient numbers to qualify for the new Formula 2. Immediately, the possibility of producing a 'small' Ferrari was reopened and the Dino was the final result.

But in 1969 – two years after the Dino 206 had been introduced and just as production of the 246 model began – a crisis point was reached. For it was then that Ferrari finally confided his troubles to Giovanni Agnelli, head of the family that controlled (and still controls) Fiat. An agreement was reached by which Ferrari retained 100 per cent ownership of the racing division, but Fiat took a fifty per cent holding in the road-cars division on the undertaking that a majority shareholding would be theirs when Enzo died. Ferrari remained president of the new company, but was responsible to two new board members appointed by Fiat, who also appointed a managing director and general manager. Fiat's immense capital resources soon took effect, one of the more visible signs being a major expansion of the production facilities at Maranello.

Yet there were regrets and second thoughts. There were worries that Ferrari's name would be devalued by this association with a down-market mass-producer of ordinary family cars. There were fears that the result would be regarded as a hybrid, neither one thing nor the other. And the change from an annual output of 600–700 cars to production rates three or four times greater brought with it a certain culture shock. To an organisation that was accustomed to receiving film stars and royalty for consultations on the trim and fittings of the cars they were buying, there were many in the factory who regarded the prospect of selling a thousand or more Dinos in a single year much as a Savile Row tailor would regard churning out suits for Austin Reed.

This, then, was why Ferrari himself said it wasn't a Ferrari at all 'because its engine is a V6 not a V12'. This is why its body carried no prancing horse badges, only the word 'Dino'; this is why it was described as being *almost* a Ferrari in those early brochures.

Fortunately both for Ferrari and a happy band of enthusiast owners, those anxieties proved to be wholly unfounded and the Dino became one of the most highly acclaimed Ferraris ever built.

THE LAYOUT

If you're not familiar with automotive engineering you may wonder why on earth the designers of the Ferrari Dino chose such a peculiar location for its power unit: it lies behind the driver and passenger but ahead of the rear wheels. As already mentioned, a layout of this kind means that the Ferrari Dino is what is rather misleadingly described as a 'mid-engined' car — misleading because the engine is not located in its exact middle.

This configuration is partly a consequence of a phase in the natural evolution of the car which began in the twenties when certain forward-thinking engineers began to criticise the conventional layout of the day involving a front engine driving the rear wheels via a long propeller shaft. One school of thought held that engine and transmission should be grouped together at the front to drive the front wheels, and the result was such cars as the Citroen Light 15, the 2CV, and later the Mini. The rival school of thought felt that the engine and transmission should be grouped at the back of the car to drive the rear wheels, and the result was the Volkswagen Beetle, Porsche 911 and many other rear-engined cars.

But although a successful rear-engined

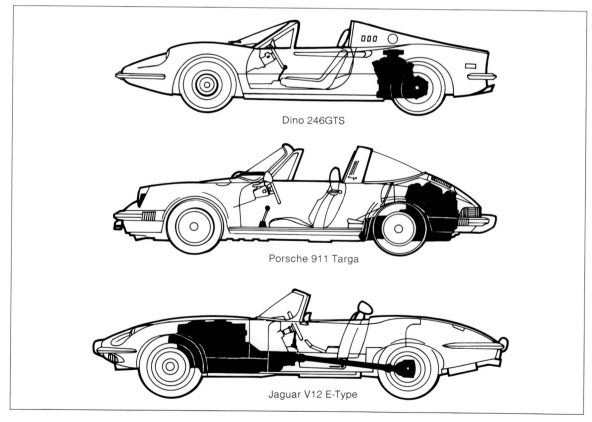

Dino 246GTS

Porsche 911 Targa

Jaguar V12 E-Type

Note how the power unit of the rear-engined Porsche 911 overhangs the rear wheels, whereas the power unit of the mid-engined Dino is mounted much further forward. The front-engined Jaguar V12 E-Type is shown for comparison.

Mid-engined cars and packaging

The mid-engine layout is very wasteful of space – to use modern jargon, it's bad for 'packaging'. Considered as a two-seater, by the standards of other mid-engined cars, the Dino has excellent accommodation, with plenty of leg-room for tall drivers and passengers and enough luggage space in its rear boot for a long journey. But set against a family saloon of the old-fashioned sort, let alone a modern space-efficient front-wheel drive car, the amount of usable room inside a Dino in relation to its exterior dimensions is very poor. The point is made by comparing the Dino's carrying capacity with that of a contemporary Ford Cortina which was of almost exactly the same overall length. Whereas the Cortina could accommodate four people and quite a lot of luggage, the Dino will only carry two people and less luggage. This is partly because the available luggage space is reduced in volume by its division into two regions – behind the engine and ahead of it – and partly because a front compartment accommodates an engine comfortably but makes a poor luggage boot due to intrusion from the footwell and the space needed to accommodate the steered front wheels. As with most rear-engined and mid-engined cars, for example, the Dino's front boot is almost entirely filled by the spare wheel.

racing car, the Auto Union, had appeared in the thirties, the precedent it set was not followed in mainstream racing for the first decade after the Second World War. Not, that is, until the products of the tiny Cooper Cars company began to have an impact. The little 500cc racers they built were all rear-engined, mostly because they were based on a rear-engined road car, the Fiat 500, and when they graduated to more powerful single-seaters and to sports-racing cars it was natural to retain the same layout for some of them; there was no elaborate design theory behind this decision, it just happened that way. Attitudes changed from derision to respect when these cars began to win Grand Prix races, and reluctantly, Ferrari eventually began to make use of their layout.

It was at about this time that designers began to look at cars of the Cooper sort more closely. They soon realised that whereas the power units of true rear-engined cars like the Volkswagen Beetle and Porsche 911 hang out behind the rear wheels, the power units of this new breed of racing car lay well forward of the rear wheels (as, in fact, had the engine of the pre-war Grand Prix Auto Union). Gradually such cars became known as 'mid-engined' ('central-engined' in most Continental languages). And inherent in this new term lay an awareness that the relatively small forward shift in the car's centre of gravity was enough to give a mid-engined car most of the advantages of a rear-engined car with few of its disadvantages.

Thus in a mid-engined car there is sufficient weight on the rear wheels for good traction in slippery conditions or under hard acceleration, yet not so much as to make the tail tend to wag the dog at the limit of adhesion. Conversely, the load on the front wheels is small enough to allow light, precise and direct steering without power assistance, despite the use of large, fat tyres. Another advantage of the mid-engined car is that it can be made fundamentally more responsive to changes in direction than either a front-engined or a rear-engined car because the concentration of its major masses well within its wheelbase reduces its 'polar moment of inertia' or 'flywheelness' about a vertical axis through its centre of gravity. In other words, it is easier to change direction by the steering.

Against these advantages must be set two disadvantages. The first is that the mid-engine configuration makes very poor use of the space available within a motorcar of given length. This is of no great consequence for a sporting two-seater, but the second disadvantage, the poor engine accessibility,

The Porsche 911 was probably the most threatening of all the Dino's competitors. This rear-engined classic remains in production after more than twenty-five years.

is more serious. The Dino's engine is barely visible beneath its hinged louvred cover, and many simple servicing jobs are difficult to perform as a result of its location.

THE SHAPE

Yet another story lies behind the Ferrari Dino's beautiful and extraordinary shape. Its true beginnings lie as far back as the early fifties when Enzo Ferrari embarked upon an association with Pinin Farina, the prominent Italian stylist and coachbuilder. Pinin Farina was soon to change both his family and his company name to Pininfarina, and

his son Sergio took over from him after his death in 1966, but the connection with Ferrari endures to this day.

The original agreement was completely informal and based on mutual respect, but whereas before the agreement Ferrari used a number of coachbuilders, including Bertone, Vignale and Touring of Milan, after it almost all Ferraris were styled by Pininfarina. Increasingly, too, the production versions of the Pininfarina designs were built by Scaglietti, a small Modenese company which became a wholly owned subsidiary of Ferrari and which is located not far from its Maranello works. Many beautiful cars were the fruits of this co-operation, but apart from the Dino itself, the most notable perhaps included the 250GT Berlinetta short-wheelbase car of 1959–1962, the 275GTB and 275GTB/4 of 1964–1967 and the 365GTB/4 Daytona of 1968–1973.

In the early sixties Pininfarina, along with a number of other designers and manufacturers, was facing up to the new challenges presented by the adoption of the mid-engine layout for road cars. The first of these lay in understanding that the configuration is not well suited to the accommodation of more than two seats (or perhaps three abreast as in the Matra Bagheera/Murena). Ingenious solutions to this drawback have been proposed, including the staggered third seat of the experimental Rover/Alvis BS and the arrangement of the Bertone Trapeze styling exercise in which the rear passengers were placed on either side of the engine with their legs outboard of the driver and front passenger. And 2 + 2 mid-engined cars have been produced, of course, including Ferrari's own 308GT4 and Mondial, but usually with rear seats that are suitable only for small children.

This limitation is of no great consequence, however, since the only sensible reason for adopting the mid-engine layout is to endow an out-and-out, uncompromising sports car with the ultimate in roadholding, handling and traction. But even the two occupants of a sports car need luggage space, and in a mid-engined car this can only be provided in a boot behind the engine, since the space in the front boot is mostly taken up by the footwell, the steered front wheels and the spare wheel. It was to provide space for this boot that the Dino's engine, originally orientated longitudinally (see Chapter 2) in early prototypes, was turned through a right angle to lie transversely.

The designers who considered these factors were quick to grasp that a two-seater mid-engined car with a boot behind the power unit could have a very odd appearance in side view: the great length of the rear deck in

Enzo Ferrari and a concerned-looking security guard before the entrance to the Ferrari factory at Modena.

relation to the small central cockpit could make it look out of proportion and rather like a pickup truck unless some stylistic feature were introduced to compensate. The easy answer is to give the car a conventional glassed-in fastback shape as was done for the Lotus Esprit. But this can lead to noise, visibility and cooling problems. The more usual solution, therefore, was to add a pair of fairings – sometimes described as sail panels or buttresses – running back into the rear deck from each side of the back window. By moving the lateral centre of aerodynamic pressure rearwards, fairings of this sort also help to improve stability in crosswinds.

In many cases these fairings ruined threequarter rear visibility, making it almost impossible to see both ways at heavily angled T-junctions, the original Lotus

Europa being one of the worst offenders. For the Dino, however, Pininfarina solved the problem brilliantly. The first part of the solution involved making the external surface of the forward part of each rear fairing into a small window which lies just behind the side window of the door. The second, unique, part was to fit a reverse-curvature rear screen with ends that sweep backwards to form part of the *inner* surfaces of the rear fairings. In this way the fairing is transparent where it needs to be and threequarter rear visibility is not seriously impaired. (The arrangement doesn't work quite so well in GTS versions for which the outer parts of the rear fairings are solid.)

After the rear screen arrangement, the most striking features of the body are perhaps the flutes in the doors and rear flanks and the ducts to which they lead.

These are a straight translation from the racing practice of the day, and admit air to the engine compartment. At the front the bodywork dips down well below the front wheel arches and recessed headlamps to form a low and aerodynamically penetrating nose incorporating a small elliptical opening which admits air both to the front-mounted radiator and to the heating and ventilation system. The apertures in the front bonnet lid allow hot air to escape, and the plastic headlamp fairings that are sometimes seen were an option for the UK market only.

Despite being reasonably easy to get into and climb out of, and despite having an acceptable ground clearance, the Dino as a whole is amazingly low, its overall height being a mere 45 inches (114cm). In most other respects the shape of the car defies analysis: it is simply an outstanding piece of sculpture.

2 Birth

Outstanding road cars very seldom start from a clean sheet of paper on the drawing board to be created new from the ground upwards in every respect. Like their more ordinary brethren, the great classics are usually the product of a long period of gradual development. But although the Ferrari Dino evolved in just this way, it differs from most other cars in owing its existence more to the demands of racing than to the requirements of the marketplace. The best account of its slow conception, gestation and birth is to be found, untainted by the hindsight of the historian, in such contemporary sources as the pages of *Motor, Autocar* and other magazines of the period in which a fascinating story gradually builds up.

Thus the motoring press first became aware of the thinking that ultimately led to the Dino in January 1964 at Ferrari's annual press conference when a new Formula 2 car was said to be under development, though no details were given. A year later Ferrari told journalists that initial plans for a 1-litre car had quickly been rendered obsolete by changes in the formula. The latest regulations for the new Formula 2, planned to start in 1967, now demanded the use of 1.6-litre engines derived from homologated (approved) GT (Gran Turismo) units of similar capacity. Accordingly, Ferrari announced his plans to build a new GT car, the Dino 168 which would be powered by a 1.6-litre V8 engine that could later be used

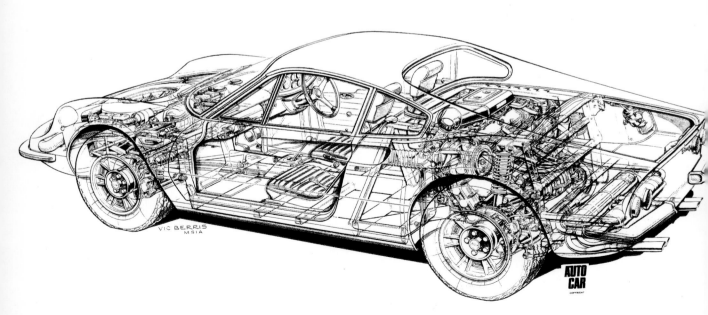

Cutaway drawing of the Dino 246GT.

*The first mid-engined, non-racing Dino was this distinctive,
low-slung prototype shown at Paris in 1965. Note the knock-off
wheels, the full hatchback revealing the longitudinally-mounted
V6 engine and the non-circular tail-lamps — very unusual for a
Ferrari.*

The Dino Berlinetta GT, shown at the Turin Show of November 1966. Like its predecessor of the year before it was very low-slung in appearance, but the basic design had evolved considerably and the car was much closer to the production version which followed.

for the new Formula 2 (see separate story — page 41).

But the formula was soon to change again. The capacity limit was still 1.6 litres, but engines must have no more than six cylinders and be based on a production unit installed in at least 500 cars. In March 1965 Italy's response to this challenge was a joint Fiat-Ferrari announcement that Fiat would be building Ferrari-designed V6 engines in the necessary numbers for a car of their own, and that the same units would power two 166 Dino GT cars that had been entered for Le Mans. A few weeks afterwards, when details of the new engine were released, its parentage became apparent, for it not only shared the 65deg bank angle and four-camshaft valvegear of the original 1956 Dino V6 power unit, but also the 77m bore dimensions of several of its variants. The stroke dimension of 57 was new, though, and

gave a capacity of 1,592cc, just within the planned formula's limit. A 2-litre 86×57mm version of this engine, developing 218bhp was soon developed, and was fitted to the open Dino 206P sports prototype with which Ludovico Scarfiotti won the 1965 European Hillclimb Championship. With redesigned combustion chambers and a lower compression ratio the same 2-litre V6 engine was also used for the successor to the Dino 166, the 206S which looked like a scaled-down version of the much more powerful 4-litre Ferrari 330P3 sports-racers.

MOTOR SHOW PROTOTYPES

It was around one of the mid-engined cars developed in this way that Pininfarina built their Dino Berlinetta styling exercise which appeared in October 1965 at the Paris Motor Show. This impressively low and sleek Pininfarina car was the first direct precursor of the road-going Dino, similar to the final version in some important respects, quite different in others. Already, though, its bodywork incorporated two of the most distinctive styling features: the recessed flanks leading to air scoops in the rear wings, and the rear buttresses or fairings, glazed externally, and with their inner surfaces partly formed by the backward sweeping ends of a reverse-curvature rear screen.

But the treatment was very different at the front where the fairings over the wheels projected well above a large, flat and very low bonnet area, giving the car the acutely 'underslung' appearance characteristic of the sports-racers of a few years before.

Further differences to the car that eventually went into production involved the four head-lamps flanking a wide air intake and the decorative strips which divided the flutes recessed into each flank. More important, however, was the design of the back of the car, where despite the absence of a luggage boot, a rear deck of great length was enforced by the longitudinal orientation of the engine ahead of the rear wheels and the gearbox hanging out behind them.

Just over a year later, at the Turin Show of November 1966, the design had further crystallised in a second Pininfarina styling exercise, the Dino Berlinetta GT. Though still very low, it had a higher, more practical roofline, and a frontal treatment very close to that of the production car with two headlamps recessed into the front wings

The Fiat Dino pre-empted its Ferrari namesake by a whole year when it appeared at the Turin Show of 1966. Although an attractive sports car, it was clearly no match for the car still being developed at Modena.

behind plastic fairings on either side of a small elliptical air intake. Enclosing 14in (35.5cm) instead of 15in (38cm) wheels, the front wings protuded upwards less than before, and were more smoothly integrated into the bonnet area between them. As for the production car, small slots in the hinged lid of this bonnet matched the louvres in the engine cover at the rear. The recesses in the flanks, however, retained their divider strips. More significantly the rear deck — formed from a very large hinged cover — was just as long as before, since it still covered a longitudinally-orientated engine and gearbox. At the same show Pininfarina also showed a larger car, based on the Ferrari 365P and notable for its three-abreast seating.

Yet another year passed before the packaging deficiency of the Dino Berlinetta GT was seen to be resolved in a third car, the Dino 206GT which appeared in November 1967, again at the Turin Show. No longer just a Pininfarina styling exercise, this car had been given the practicality it needed by Ferrari whose engineers had turned the engine through a right angle to lie transversely, thus releasing enough space for a luggage boot of reasonable size behind it. One result of this change was to split the one-piece long rear deck into a pair of hinged covers: a small louvred cover over the engine compartment, and immediately behind that a slightly larger lid for the rear boot. Another consequence of the modification was to raise the rear deck slightly, but following wind-tunnel tests at Turin Polytechnic this was found to reduce drag and improve high-speed stability. By raking the windscreen back three more degrees, the drag was further reduced, one source quoting a final drag coefficient of 0.362 — not bad for a period in which a typical value for a road car was 0.45 (a later UK measurement was to yield a value of 0.34). The side flutes had lost their unnecessary divider strips by this time, but the transparent plastic fairings over the headlamps remained.

At the same show Pininfarina exhibited another variation on the theme, the Dino Prototipo Competizione. But although it shared some features of the road car such as the rear air intakes and reverse-curvature screen, it had little influence on the evolution of the 206GT, being a track-orientated exercise with gullwing doors and a tail-mounted wing.

THE 206GT

The Dino 206GT which appeared at the 1967 Turin show was in all major respects the car that was first offered for sale to the general public — it was what the Ferrari and Pininfarina engineers described as the 'ante-prototype' or the final development car immediately preceding the first production prototype. Another year, though, was to elapse before many cars were actually built.

The watercooled light alloy V6 engine that powered the new car bore a rather distant relationship to the original Formula 2 Dino unit of 1956, having been extensively redesigned by Ferrari engineer Franco Rocchi and further modified for ease of production by Aurelio Lampredi, formerly of Ferrari, but then working for Fiat. In addition to the 65deg bank angle already mentioned, however, the revised engine did retain the staggered cylinder banks, the six-throw four-bearing crankshaft designed to give even firing intervals and the four camshafts of the original design. As before, too, the crankcase and blocks were formed from a single light-alloy casting into which cast iron cylinder liners were inserted.

But with a stroke of 57mm and a bore of 86mm — giving a capacity of 1,987cc — the cylinder dimensions of the new Dino engine were highly oversquare. And following the design thinking of the day, the two valves of each hemispherical combustion chamber were set at a smaller included angle (of 47deg) than before, while single sparking plugs were fitted. The four camshafts were driven by chains and sprockets and actuated the valves via bucket tappets incorporating shims with which the clearance could be adjusted. The inlet camshaft on the rearmost bank of cylinders drove the distributor which dispensed the sparks generated by a dual ignition arrangement composed of a new Marelli 'Dinoplex' electronic ignition system and a conventional alternative fitted as a standby that could be selected by swapping connectors. A lubricating pump driven off the nose of the crankshaft drew oil from a conventional wet sump at the bottom of the crankcase to circulate it through the engine via a small oil/water heat exchanger mounted in the engine compartment. Mixture was sucked in through three twin-choke Weber 40 DCN 14 carburetters and the claimed output for the engine as fitted to the Ferrari Dino was 180bhp at 8,000rpm on a compression ratio of 9.3:1. (A lower output was claimed for the Fiat Dino version of the power unit — see page 38.)

By setting this high-performance V6 sideways in the chassis, the Ferrari engineers liberated a good deal of useful space, but created a transmission problem. They solved it with an ingenious arrangement which is both neat and compact. From a clutch mounted on the end of the crankshaft, the drive is passed downwards via three transfer gears to a quill shaft designed to absorb torsional shock loads. This quill shaft is coupled directly to the input of a five-speed all-synchromesh gearbox which forms part of a self-contained transaxle mounted beneath and behind the engine. It also incorporates a pair of final drive gears and a limited-slip differential linked to a pair of flanges to which the drive shafts are bolted. This transaxle is bolted to the bottom of the crankcase, part of its cast aluminium casing forming the engine sump. But behind that sump lies a second and separate sump for the gearbox, the lubricating oil of which is circulated by the transaxle's own pump. Yet the engine's centre of gravity is only slightly raised, since the gearbox sits behind rather than beneath it, its shafts lying not far below the crankshaft centreline. Equally, the transaxle nestles beneath the overhang of the rearmost cylinder bank, adding very little to the longitudinal space taken up by the engine.

As cutaway profile drawings of the complete car clearly show, this arrangement positioned its two heaviest elements behind the driver and passenger yet ahead of the front wheels and concentrated them into a group of quite remarkable compactness. One result was to create rather more usable space in a Dino than in other mid-engined cars of similar size, legroom being ample for all but the exceptionally tall, while the rear boot is big enough to take several cases of reasonable size.

Helped by the location of the radiator and (full-sized) spare wheel right at the front of the car, the arrangement also contributed to a relatively conservative rearward distribution of weight which put enough load (about fifty-five per cent of the total unladen weight for the 206) on the rear wheels for good traction under hard acceleration in slippery conditions, but not so much as to introduce the tail-happy behaviour and sharp oversteer characteristics which are typical of a rear-engined — rather than mid-engined — car at the limit of adhesion. Yet at the same time the configuration relieved the front wheels of sufficient weight to allow light, precise steering without power assistance despite the use of fat tyres, and without removing enough weight to cause premature lock-up under braking in the wet.

A further effect of this concentration of masses within the wheelbase was to create the low polar moment of inertia already mentioned in Chapter 1 (see separate story — page 47) which makes the car so agile and quick to respond when driving fast on a twisty road. Too low a polar moment tends to make a car twitchy and nervous, but here

Specification

	206GT	246GT
Engine		
Block material	Light alloy	Cast iron
Head material	Light alloy	Light alloy
Cylinders	6 in 65deg V	
Cooling	Water	
Bore and Stroke	86×57mm	92.5×60mm
Capacity	1,987cc	2,418cc
Main bearings	4	
Valves	2 per cyl; dohc per bank	
Compression ratio	9.3:1	9.0:1
Carburetters	3 Weber 40 DCN 14	3 Weber 40 DCN F/7 (F/13 from chassis no 02132 on; F/19 & 20 with US emission control system)
Max power (net)	180bhp @ 8,000rpm	195bhp @ 7,600rpm
Max revs	8,000rpm	7,800rpm
Max torque	137 lb ft @ 6,500rpm	165.5 lb ft @ 5,500rpm

Transmission

Clutch — Single dry plate; diaphragm spring; mechanically operated

Internal gearbox ratios

	206GT & 246GT up to chassis no. 02130	246GT 02132 onwards
Top	0.857:1	0.896:1
4th	1.125:1	1.200:1
3rd	1.524:1	1.619:1
2nd	2.117:1	2.235:1
1st	3.077:1	3.231:1
Reverse	2.667:1	3.000:1
Transfer gears	33/27=1.222:1 } 4.430:1	33/30=1.100:1 } 4.206:1
Final drive	58/16=3.625:1 }	65/17=3.824:1 }

Suspension and steering

Front	Independent by unequal-length double wishbones with coil springs, telescopic dampers and an anti-roll bar	
Rear	Independent by unequal-length double wishbones with coil springs, telescopic dampers and an anti-roll bar	
Steering	Rack and pinion	
Tyres	185 VR 14	205 VR 14
Wheels	Light alloy; centrelock	Light or magnesium alloy; centre lock, then 5-bolt fixing; Fiat or Chromodora
Rim size	6.5in (165mm)	

	206GT	246GT
Brakes		
Type	Servo-assisted ventilated discs with front/rear split and rear pressure-relief valve	
Size	Girling 10.6in diameter all round to chassis no. 01116; Ate 10.6 in front, 10.9 in rear, from chassis no. 01118	
Dimensions (in/cm)		
Track		
Front	56.1/142.5	55.8/141.7
Rear	55.12/140.0	56.8/144.3
Wheelbase	89.76/228.0	92.3/234.0
Overall length	163.38/415.0	166.7/423.5
Overall width	66.93/170.0	67.0/170.2
Overall height	43.90/111.5	45.0/114.3
Ground clearance	5.12/13.0	5.5/14.0
Unladen weight (with fuel for approx 50 miles)	22.4cwt/1140kg	23.3cwt/1186kg
Front/rear weight distribution	45/55	43/57

again the forward location of the radiator and spare wheel helps, increasing the value just enough to avoid instability without significantly reducing response.

The compact engine/transmission unit sat in a chassis of elliptical-section and rectangular-section steel tubes built up above floor level at the front to support the suspension and at the rear to support engine and suspension. A large central tube added stiffness and carried various services. A pair of thermostatically-controlled electric fans maintained the flow of air through the front-mounted radiator at low speeds and in hot weather. In addition to the spare wheel already mentioned, the battery and the brake servo were also mounted at the front of the car.

Adopting a racing design practice of the period (and one which is maintained to this day) the 206GT was given independent suspension for all four wheels by unequal-length double wishbones. At the time many road cars — such as the Mini, the Citroen DS and the Triumph 2000 — had independent suspension all round, and quite a number were fitted with double-wishbone systems at the front, but very few had them at the rear. The space taken up by the necessary pivot points plus the cost and complexity of the arrangement ruled it out for most ordinary cars. In this respect, therefore, the Dino was — and remains — unusual.

The suspension system was completed by straightforward coil springs encircling Koni dampers, acting on the lower wishbones at the front, but on the upper part of the hub-carrier at the rear to clear the drive shafts; anti-roll bars were fitted at both ends of the car. The steering was by rack and pinion — a first for Ferrari who until then had lagged behind contemporary design standards with their adherence to worm and peg steering systems. Massive ventilated disc brakes were fitted all round, actuated with vacuum servo assistance via a tandem master cylinder through a front hydraulic circuit and a separate rear hydraulic circuit incorporating a pressure-relief valve to prevent premature rear-wheel lockup. Knock-off alloy wheels,

A superb example of the 1967 Fiat Dino Spider.

mounted on centrelock hubs, were fitted, and had 6.5in (16.51cm) rims supporting 185-section tyres at front and rear.

All these mechanical assemblies were clothed in the flamboyant, curvacious bodywork already described – and it was made entirely of aluminium. Its distinctive details included four circular tail lights, small quarter bumpers at each corner of the car and an exposed fuel filler cap in the left-hand rear buttress. For the production models, the plastic headlamp covers were

Third in line (left): *the Dino 206GT, which was launched at the Turin Show of November 1967 and was virtually identical to the production car.*

dropped, and the little side-windows in the rear buttresses became swivelling quarter-lights. A small 'Dino' badge at the front and a similar 'Dino GT' badge at the rear were the only means of identification.

THE FIAT DINOS

Fiat pre-empted their partners by more than a year when they introduced their own Dino, powered by the same V6 engine, but very different in character, at the Turin Show of 1966 when the Ferrari Dino was still only in the second stage of its evolution. Perhaps Ferrari insisted that the two models should not compete too closely, for the Fiat Dino, though an attractive and exciting car, was no rival to its namesake from Maranello.

The Fiat Dino was assigned a lower place in the pecking order by being a conventional front-engined car, with, in its original form, a simple, even old-fashioned, design incorporating double-wishbone suspension at the front but a live axle at the rear. The car first appeared as a Spider, with open bodywork by Pininfarina, but a Bertone-styled 2 + 2 coupe version was added a few months later at the Geneva Show of March 1967.

Careful design had made it easy to adapt the V6 engine to the different transmission arrangement. In the Fiat application, an ordinary sump was substituted for the Ferrari transaxle, and a conventional five-speed gearbox, derived from a unit developed for the Fiat 124, was bolted to the back of the engine, which was longitudinally aligned. Fiat's version of this power unit was said to develop no more than 160bhp, casting doubt on Ferrari's claim of 180bhp for his variant, since it was identical in every respect to its rival except for carburetter settings.

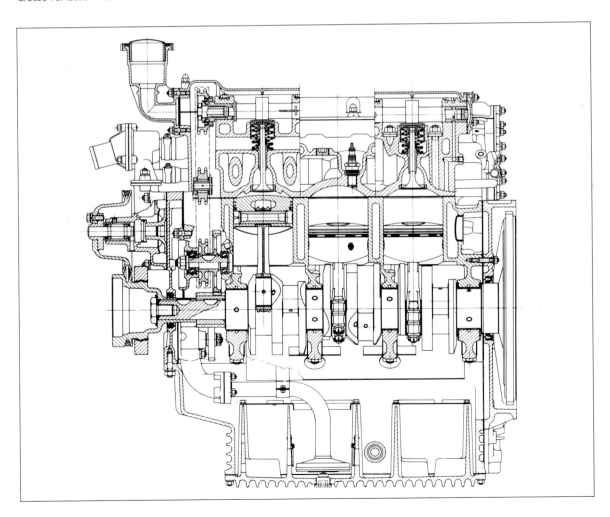

246 engine.

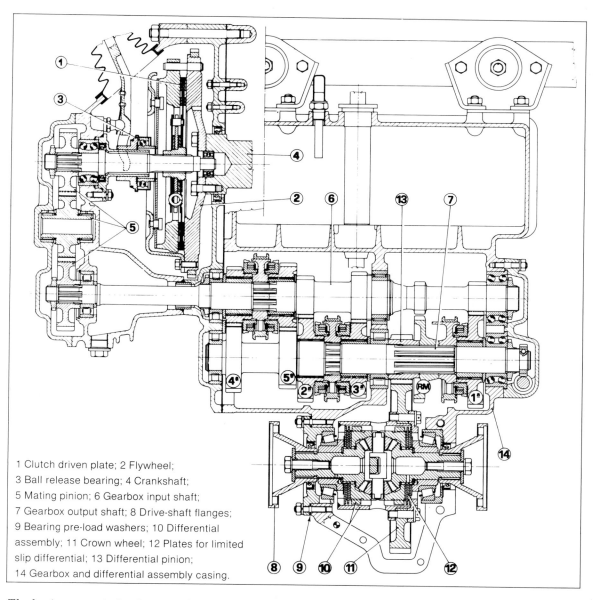

1 Clutch driven plate; 2 Flywheel;
3 Ball release bearing; 4 Crankshaft;
5 Mating pinion; 6 Gearbox input shaft;
7 Gearbox output shaft; 8 Drive-shaft flanges;
9 Bearing pre-load washers; 10 Differential
assembly; 11 Crown wheel; 12 Plates for limited
slip differential; 13 Differential pinion;
14 Gearbox and differential assembly casing.

*The basic transmission layout. The gear cluster layout and
ratios changed during the car's production run.*

In 1969 the Fiat Dinos were given independent rear suspension when they received the uprated version of the V6 engine (see 246GT) with its cast iron cylinder block and capacity of 2.4 litres. (See Chapter 6 for full details of the Fiat Dinos.)

THE 206GT IN PRODUCTION

When a big manufacturer launches a new model at an international motor show, numerous prototypes will have been built

Dino 246GT (1973).

long before, and the production lines will already be active. But in the late sixties Ferrari often revealed the existence of new cars before they were fully developed. In general this approach seldom created difficulties, since each new model in the mainstream range of V12 cars was usually only a modest advance on its immediate predecessor.

The Dino, however, was radically different from any Ferrari that had then been designed for public roads. So even though the prototype displayed at the Turin Show of November 1967 fixed the design of the 206GT in most of its details as well as its general conception, progress towards its series production was at first slow.

By July 1968, though, eight months after that Turin Show launch, journalist, Le Mans winner and former Grand Prix driver Paul Frère was able to record a trip, with Enzo Ferrari himself at the wheel, in one of the three production prototypes that had then been built. A few months later, in January 1969, Paul returned to Maranello to find that 206GTs were being built at the rate of one per day.

At that time Ferrari hadn't even considered the possibility of making cars available to the press for road tests. The low volume of their production made it difficult, if not impossible, to set a car aside for such purposes, and in any case the rich and the famous queued up to buy the company's products without any help – or hindrance – that journalists might provide. But during his January visit to Italy Paul Frère was able to borrow a Dino, the first true production car, owned by Sergio Pininfarina, and subject it to a short test. Despite the aluminium used for its engine and its bodywork, he found it quite heavy, turning the scales at 2,510lb or 22.4cwt (1,140kg) unladen except for about

These views of the 246's engine demonstrate the extreme inaccessibility of its location. It is notoriously hard to work on when in situ.

Ferrari model designations

Over the years Ferrari have designated their different models with three entirely different numbering systems, which can make quick identification of a particular car a difficult business for a newcomer. The first system devised applied mostly to V12 cars and used the capacity in cubic centimetres of a single cylinder. Thus a 166 had a 2-litre V12 because 166×12 = 1,992cc, while similarly a 250 was a 3-litre V12-engined car, a 330 was a 4-litre V12 car, a 750 a 4-litre four-cylinder car, and so on.

With the introduction of six and eight cylinder cars came a different system. Here, the first two numbers represent the capacity and the last one the number of cylinders, so that a 206 car is powered by a 2-litre six-cylinder engine, the 246 by a 2.4-litre six, the 308 by a 3.0-litre eight, the 512 by a 5.0-litre V12, etc. Suffix numbers sometimes indicate the number of seats as in 308GT4, or sometimes the number of camshafts as in 275GTB4.

Thirdly and finally, two cars were designated solely by their capacity: the 400 (4-litre) Superamerica and the 500 (5-litre) Superfast.

five gallons (22.73L) of fuel. Even so, it managed a 0–60mph (96.5kph) acceleration time of 7.5 sec and a top speed of 140mph (225kph). Although usually sober in his assessments, Paul made his enthusiasm for the car quite clear with such statements as: 'In fact, crisp, beautifully balanced handling and quite exceptional roadholding are the Dino's major virtues . . .' (For more details see Chapter 3.)

But in another comment was to be found a hint of the short production life that was to be the fate of the 206GT: 'Of production 2-litre cars, only the Porsche 911S can just match these figures . . .' Unfortunately for Ferrari, the Porsche 911S was not only widely perceived to be the immediate rival of the 206GT, but was also known to be getting a more powerful 2.2-litre engine. Almost as

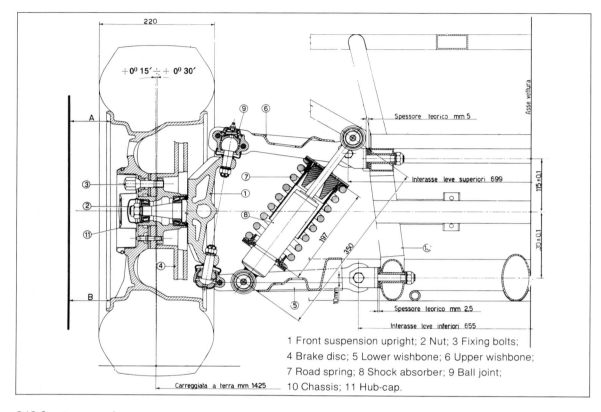

1 Front suspension upright; 2 Nut; 3 Fixing bolts;
4 Brake disc; 5 Lower wishbone; 6 Upper wishbone;
7 Road spring; 8 Shock absorber; 9 Ball joint;
10 Chassis; 11 Hub-cap.

246 front suspension.

soon as the 206GT began to appear on the roads, however, Ferrari had understood the danger and, with Fiat, began to make plans for a more powerful version of the Dino. So when Porsche introduced their bigger engine in the autumn of 1969, production of the 206GT was already being phased out. Since the Ferrari chassis numbering system might almost have been designed to confuse, estimates of the total number of cars produced vary. However, the best guess at the time of writing (summer 1989) is that 150 206GTs were built altogether, all with left-hand drive, and it is known with some certainty that only five of these were imported new into Britain.

THE 246GT

The weakness of the 2-litre V6 Dino engine was not merely that its claimed maximum power of 180bhp at 8,000rpm (in its Ferrari application) was about to become outclassed. It was also sadly lacking in pull at low revs, the peak torque value of 137lb ft for the same variant of the engine being reached at a ridiculously high 6,500rpm. Similar criticisms applied to the less powerful Fiat version of the engine.

In response to this situation Fiat and Ferrari collaborated to introduce an enlarged version of their engine with bore and stroke dimensions of 92.5×60mm, raising the capacity to 2,418cc. To cut costs and simplify production, cast iron was at the same time substituted for light alloy as the cylinder block material. But light alloy was retained for the cylinderheads, and in every other detail of its layout and construction the new engine was simply a scaled-up version of the old one. Breathing through three 40 DCN/7F Weber carburetters it developed 15bhp more than before in its Ferrari form, and at lower revs: 195bhp at 7,600rpm. Maximum torque was increased to 165.5lb ft at a more sensible 5,500rpm. For the Fiat variant the equivalent figures were 180bhp at 6,600rpm and 159lb ft of torque at 4,600rpm.

With this enlarged and more powerful engine, introduced at the Turin Show of November 1969, came major changes to the cars themselves. As already mentioned, the Fiat Dinos gained independent rear suspension (for more details see Chapter 5) but the major alteration to the Ferrari Dino was the adoption of steel instead of aluminium for its bodywork. The car grew slightly, too, gaining 2.4in (6cm) in the wheelbase and 3.7in (9.4cm) in overall length. In addition, the chassis was modified in the region of the central tube to make a right-hand drive model possible. Externally, though, the new car was difficult to distinguish from the old one, the only significant visual difference being the concealment of the fuel filler cap in a recess covered by a small flap in the bodywork.

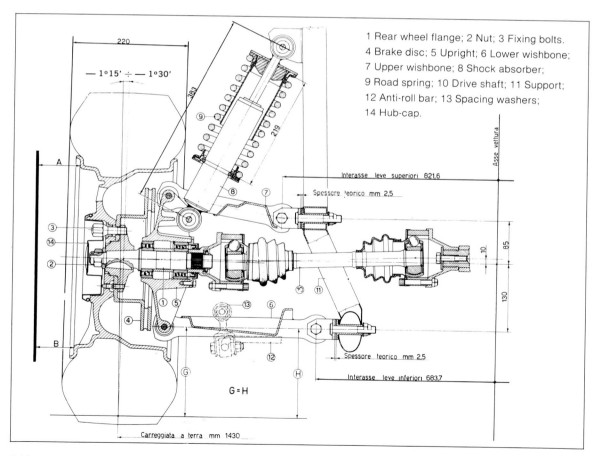

1 Rear wheel flange; 2 Nut; 3 Fixing bolts.
4 Brake disc; 5 Upright; 6 Lower wishbone;
7 Upper wishbone; 8 Shock absorber;
9 Road spring; 10 Drive shaft; 11 Support;
12 Anti-roll bar; 13 Spacing washers;
14 Hub-cap.

246 rear suspension.

The acclaimed 2.4-litre V6 engine which powers the Dino 246GT, and is set transversely in the chassis.

Dino 246GTS (1972).

Dino 246GTS (1974) (above).

A fair-sized boot is located behind the Dino's engine, covered by an independent hatch (below).

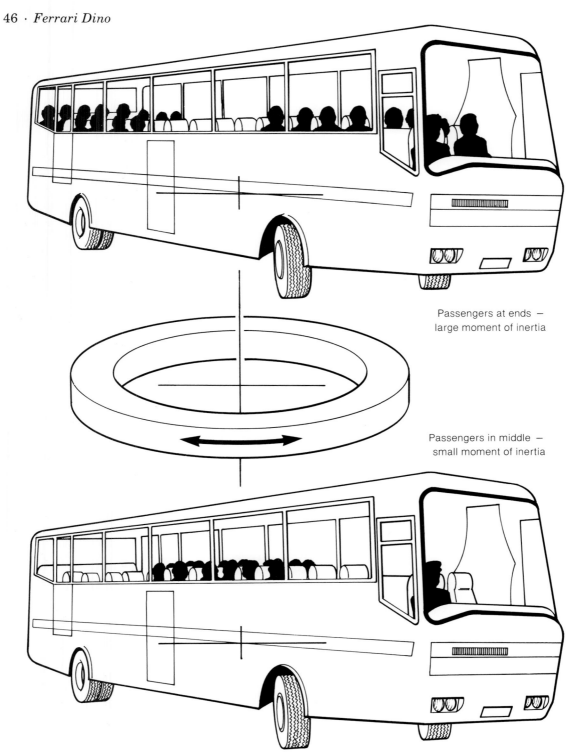

Passengers at ends —
large moment of inertia

Passengers in middle —
small moment of inertia

How the disposition of passengers can affect the 'flywheelness'
or moment of inertia of a coach.

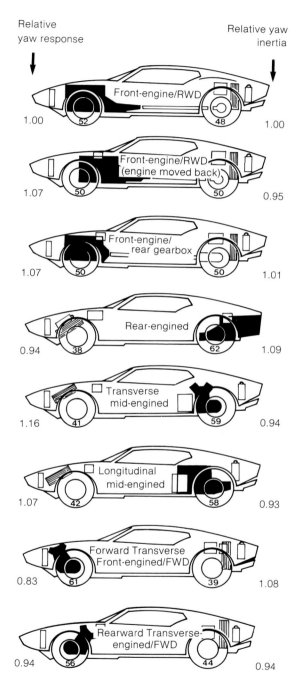

Relative yaw response

Relative yaw inertia

Front-engine/RWD
1.00   52   48   1.00

Front-engine/RWD
(engine moved back)
1.07   50   50   0.95

Front-engine/
rear gearbox
1.07   50   50   1.01

Rear-engined
0.94   38   62   1.09

Transverse
mid-engined
1.16   41   59   0.94

Longitudinal
mid-engined
1.07   42   58   0.93

Forward Transverse
Front-engined/FWD
0.83   61   39   1.08

Rearward Transverse-
engined/FWD
0.94   56   44   0.94

Layouts compared: eight different configurations and their associated relative polar moments of inertia and yaw responses to a steering input.

Polar moment of inertia

A car's polar moment of inertia defines how big it is as a flywheel about a vertical axis through its centre of gravity. We can get a crude idea of its influence on handling by imagining ourselves playing with a toy bus partially occupied by lead soldiers. If we move all the soldiers to the front and to the rear of the bus leaving a gap in the middle, we will have given it a large polar moment of inertia which means that a large torque or twisting effort will be required to spin it on a polished floor. Once spinning, however, it will have a large angular momentum and will not be easily slowed. Clearly such a characteristic will tend to make a vehicle sluggish and unresponsive in corners and will not be desirable for a sporting car.

If we now move all the soldiers to the centre of the bus, it will be much easier to spin but also more easily stopped from spinning. Thus a given disturbing torque will impart a high angular acceleration to a car with a low polar moment of inertia so that it may end up being deflected through 180deg or more before the driver has time to react. Equally, a relatively small increase in adhesion will be sufficient to stop such a car spinning, so that while it may rapidly get 20deg out of line on a slippery patch, it may then regain its grip with such rapidity as hardly to need correction. As is usual in automotive engineering, therefore, a compromise value must be sought, but the mid-engine layout allows that value to be low enough for greater responsiveness in corners than is possible with a front-engineed car yet high enough for acceptable stability.

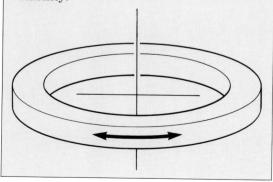

A re-trimmed car with the Daytona-style seats.

Slots in the bonnet help — rather inadequately — to let out hot air from the radiator.

The reverse-curvature rear screen which is such a distinctive feature of the Dino design.

A classic racing-style air intake; on the Dino this helps to cool the engine rather than the brakes.

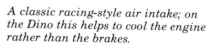

There are few visible differences between the 206 (above) and the 246 (below); only the knock-off wheels and exposed filler cap distinguish the 206. This is an early Pininfarina prototype without quarterlights. The Ferrari sticker was probably a publicity addition.

*The wheels of the 246 were secured by five nuts, unlike those of
the 206 with their 'knock-off' caps.*

These changes are often said to have increased the weight of the car by more than 300lb (135kg), but this is perhaps because the new model was being compared with an early lightweight prototype of the 206. A comparison of Paul Frère's weight for a production version of this car with the *Motor* road test figure for its steel-bodied successor suggests an increase of almost exactly 1cwt or 51kg. And certainly the net result was a small but significant improvement in performance. The engine had much more torque at low speeds and would comfortably pull maximum revs in fifth gear, giving a maximum speed of 148mph (238kph).

This, then, was the Ferrari Dino 246GT — or more correctly, just the Dino 246GT, since as before it carried no prancing horse or

The speedometer and rev-counter are partially concealed by the steering wheel (above); at least one owner has moved them to the centre of the display.

The recessed headlamp of a Dino 246 (below) has an almost animate quality when viewed in close-up.

The prancing horse (above) *was a late addition to the back of this car.*

All but the early cars had bolt-on wheels (below) *made by Fiat or Cromodora.*

Ferrari emblems, being identified only by 'Dino' and 'Dino GT' badges at front and rear as before. It arrived on the scene some four months after Fiat's acquisition of Ferrari's road-car division had been formally announced. In fact, as already mentioned in chapter 1, Fiat bought only fifty per cent of this operation, under an agreement which gave them effective control and guaranteed full ownership following Ferrari's death.

The deal was more than enough for Fiat to begin investing in the facilities at Maranello. They had already designed and supplied a tooling line for the machining and assembly of the shared engine, and were also supplying many of its parts, particularly the major castings, all of which were stamped 'Fiat'. This rapidly developing involvement speeded production of the 246 Dino, so that right-hand drive cars soon became available in Britain and in February 1970 an example was offered to *Motor* for a brief road appraisal. By the end of that year a production line for the assembly of the Fiat Dino had been laid down in an extension to Ferrari's Maranello factory, where assembly of the engine for both cars and of the Ferrari Dino was carried out.

In the middle of the following year, 1971, a car was offered to *Motor* for a full appraisal with performance figures — a landmark for its road-testers, remembered to this day. Production was then in full swing, roughly fifteen Fiat Dinos and three Ferrari Dinos being built every day. The open 246GTS model was introduced at the Geneva Show of March 1972, and in the same year became available, in both open and closed forms, on the US market with the appropriate exhaust emission control equipment. Production continued to the middle of 1974 when the car was superseded by the V8-engined 2 + 2 308GT4 announced at the Paris Show of October 1973 (see Chapter 6).

3 Reception

With its beautiful and unusual styling and its advanced design, the 206 Dino excited widespread admiration following its introduction at the Turin Show of November 1967, and the press couldn't wait to get their hands on it. 'The Dino 206,' wrote Paul Frère in *Motor,* 'is a car I desperately wanted to drive. It looks so exactly right, so beautifully balanced and logical in its conception that I just had to find out about it'.

But at that early stage in the Dino project, Ferrari regarded themselves, as already mentioned in Chapter 2, much as a London gunmaker would. Their reputation was so high that they expected their customers to come to them, not they to their customers. When princes, maharajas and film stars practically begged for the privilege of owning a Ferrari, the idea of providing a press demonstrator car was a laughable extravagance. So even the most highly respected journalists had to wait for more than a year before being able to drive a 206 Dino for themselves.

As soon as they were able to do so, however, the praise was universal and lavish. Writing in *Sports Car Graphic* Etienne Cornil described it as 'a noble thoroughbred' with 'enrapturing road behaviour'. *Car* magazine's view was that 'Rarely can a car born in the heat of competition have been so successfully adapted to road use; so well adapted is the 206GT Dino that it stands out as one of the most advanced grand touring cars of our time'. Similarly, Paul Frère enthused about its '. . . enormous cornering power, perfect balance which keeps the car in an almost perfectly neutral attitude whatever you do with the accelerator . . .'

Of all these assessments Paul Frère's was certainly the most authoritative and perceptive. Following a successful racing career which included a spell in Grand Prix and a win (with Olivier Gendebien) at Le Mans, he could (and still can, despite being in his early seventies at the time of writing) drive high-performance road or competition cars as quickly as — and often quicker than — the professional development engineers or racing drivers normally responsible for them. His training as an engineer made him analytical about performance and handling, his fluency in French, German, English and Italian helped to gain him a wide circle of friends, so that he was and still is treated as a highly-respected equal by leading figures in the European motor industry, which in those days included Rudi Uhlenhaut of Daimler-Benz, Dr Ferry Porsche and Enzo Ferrari himself.

Accordingly, let us gain a more detailed insight into the impact made by the 206 Dino on contemporary observers through the following two Paul Frère articles, both written for *Motor* , the first appearing in the issue of 6 July 1968 and the second in the issue of 25 January 1969.

ITALIAN DIARY
by Paul Frère
Reproduced from *Motor* 6 July 1968

Ferrari's Dino

Another car I was very keen to try is Ferrari's transverse-engined Dino 206GT, of which three have been completed fully developed. The production line is now being finished and it will not be long before the first series is put in hand. With its Ferrari-designed and Fiat-made 2-litre V-6 mounted across the frame in front of the rear wheels, this very low-built little two-seater coupe is one of the most handsome cars Pininfarina has designed for a long time. And it is quite practical too, as there is a lot of room inside and an acceptable luggage locker. The alloy wheels with 6½in wide rims are Fiat too but, otherwise, the car

is entirely made by Ferrari and it is much lighter and has a much lower frontal area (as well, no doubt, as a much better shape) than Fiat's Dino, which uses the same engine.

I have never known a journalist who has been given a free hand by Enzo Ferrari to take one of his cars out and find out for himself how it went, and this apparently still applies even to those who have been judged good enough to drive the works' Formula 1 and big

Details from an original Ferrari publicity brochure for the Dino 246GT.

sports cars. So, when it came to trying the Dino, we went out together and he took the wheel without comment. It is 10 years since I was last driven by the boss himself, who is now 70, but I must say, the precision, authority and speed with which this racing driver of 45 years ago handles his car are still really impressive and have not changed at all since I last rode with him. And the car itself was a revelation: with its light weight (less than a ton), low centre of gravity and very low polar moment, it corners as flat as a kipper,

seems to be perfectly neutral and is incredibly agile. Even in this light car, it is evident that the engine does not produce a lot of power below 5,000rpm but with the (Ferrari-designed and made) five-speed gear box, it is very easy to keep the revs above this, when the engine really comes into life, right up to the 8,000rpm limit. The noise level is quite acceptable, about the same as a Porsche 911, and the marvellous handling has not been achieved at the cost of comfort. As a result of the low drag, Ferrari says all three cars made

High efficiency

The mechanical features of the Dino 246/GT incorporate the latest innovations evolved from the most recent Ferrari technical research.

The 6 cylinder 65° V form engine, with a power of 195 HP at 7600 RPM, possesses flexibility and surprising agility.

The cooling circuit, lubrication and electronic ignition systems have all been improved.

The synchronized five-speed gearbox, with gear ratios which lend themselves to sporting driving, enables the engine power to be used in the best possible way, and offers outstanding acceleration.

The tubular lattice chassis is of new design, based on a classical study of rigidity and safety tests.

The spare wheel is located at the front and almost horizontally, also incorporating anti-shock elements.

Also of new design are the independent suspension units on the four wheels and on the brake circuit, having been conceived with a view to affording conditions of comfort under circumstances of high-level motoring.

A general view of the Ferrari Dino 246GTS (1973). Note the slotted rear quarterlight panels which reduce three-quarter rear visibility.

were timed at between 143 and 146mph.

For some time the car will not be exported and Ferrari, who wants to keep his firm small enough to be able to manage it all himself, is certainly not prepared to make enough cars to meet the demand there would be if it were priced to suit a production of, say 15 or 20 a day. Otherwise, this car could well give Porsche something to think about. It obviously offers a lot of possibilities for future development when you think that Chris Amon's Tasman car of 2,417cc developed 302bhp from the standard Fiat-made cylinder block — nearly twice as much as the output of the standard 2-litre engine.

CONTINENTAL DIARY
by Paul Frère

Reproduced from *Motor*
25 January 1969

Out in Ferrari's Dino

Apart from winning races, Ferrari is not very interested in any sort of publicity for his cars. He does not force them on to film stars or pop singers; he waits for them to come and buy one. And his must surely be the only factory today which not only has no Press cars (or even car), but which has never entrusted any *of its cars to a journalist, even to one who has been judged worthy of driving his racing machinery. I can understand this: whereas a man in racing overalls will always do his best to try and win and thus do justice to whatever car is entrusted to him, the same man may use his typewriter to less flattering purposes.*

Practically speaking, this means that if you want to lay your hands on a Ferrari, you must buy one (which is beyond the means of most journalists), or be very friendly with a distributor (and never ask whose car you are being given) or else have a friend who has one and is generous enough to let you try it.

Though Ferrari models change about every three years, their character, dominated by the V12 engine, does not change much and even if, compared with its contemporaries, a present day 365GT or GTB is an infinitely better car than say, a 166 Inter of 15 years ago, the jump from one model to the next is never such that its successor comes as a complete surprise. There is one exception in today's range however: the little Dino 206GT which is entirely different from anything Ferrari has produced to date. Ferrari himself, of course, will say it's not a Ferrari at all and isn't called one because its engine is a V6, not a V12. Moreover, the six-cylinder engine is centrally located and transverse, so it really has no predecessor and the Fiat Dino which shares the same (Ferrari-designed) engine is too different in its (classical) layout to provide any clue.

The Dino 206 is a car I desperately wanted to drive. It looks so exactly right, so beautifully balanced and so logical in its conception that I just had to find out about it. And the short ride I had a few months ago as Enzo Ferrari's passenger, far from satisfying my curiosity only whetted my appetite even more.

Fortunately, I did not have to buy one, for Sergio Pininfarina who designed the body (which is built by Scaglietti in Modena however) owns the first production model to be made and very kindly suggested I should take

it out for a day. The car had nearly 7,000 kilometres on the clock, but Sergio told me he had done only about half the mileage himself as so many people had come and borrowed it before me. It seems that not only mere journalists have some difficulties in obtaining a Ferrari, as the borrowers included Umberto Agnelli (Gianni's brother and Fiat vice-president) and the Fiat experimental department!

The latter were, of course, particularly interested, as the engine, basically a 1961–1964 Formula One Ferrari developed and built by Fiat is virtually identical to the one used in Fiat's own Dino. Ferrari claims 20hp more for his, but this sounds rather optimistic, as he himself says that only the carburettor settings are changed, and the exhaust system just cannot be more efficient with the space limitations imposed on it. In the 206GT, the engine is, of course, mounted transversely behind the seats, making the car a pure and uncompromising two-seater, and the whole transmission unit, made and designed by Ferrari and driven by spur gears off the crankshaft, simply bolts in place of the original sump; the lubrication systems are separate, which allows the use of a limited slip differential. The outer panels of the car are of aluminium and the floor structure is a composite tube and welded steel structure with four-wheel independent suspension by transverse wishbones and Koni suspension struts front and rear.

In spite of the widespread use of aluminium (and plastics for many invisible or covered interior fittings such as the dashboard and the spare wheel recess) the car is not light. With about five gallons of fuel, it turned the scales at 1,140kg (2,510lb), only about 50kg less than the reputedly heavy Fiat Dino Spyder which is a (admittedly very occasional) 2 + 2. So with a near identical engine and not much less weight, the Ferrari Dino derives its performance mainly from much better aerodynamics and easier, wheelspin-less take-off. The shape is obviously

Full frontal views of a GT (right) and a GTS (left). Both cars have British market plastic headlamp covers. The repose position of the wipers indicates a clap-hands action.

much better and the frontal area considerably less, bringing about an illuminating increase of the maximum speed from 125mph to 140mph and reducing the time needed to cover a kilometre from a standing start from 29.9 to 28.1 seconds. Ferrari claims even better figures than these: a 6mph higher maximum and one second less for the standing start kilometre, but these were actually achieved by one of the prototypes which weighed just a ton and had a noisier, freer exhaust system, so that the figures I obtained on the Torino-Ivrea Autostrada should be representative of the production model, and pretty good they are for a road-going 2-litre car too:

Maximum speed: *140mph*

0 to 50mph	*5.6sec.*
0 to 60	*7.5*
0 to 70	*9.8*
0 to 80	*12.2*
0 to 90	*15.3*
0 to 100	*19.2*
0 to 110	*24.0*
0 to 120	*30.6*

Standing start ¼ mile: 15.5 sec.
Standing start kilometre: 28.1 sec.

Of production 2-litre cars, only the Porsche 911S can just match these figures, and when the world's two greatest high performance specialists get equal results from cars which both set out to be two-seaters of maximum

performance compatible with a reasonably flexible 2-litre engine which does not mind being used in city traffic, this must be the limit of what you can expect today.

There is one basic difference in the concept of the two cars, however: Porsche set out to provide scanty rear accommodation for two small children or, for short distances, even for acrobatic adults, which meant they had to use an overhung rear engine. The Dino is an uncompromising two-seater with the engine located where the sufferer's seats are in the Porsche, which considerably simplifies handling problems. In fact, crisp, beautifully balanced handling and quite exceptional road holding are the Dino's major virtues: they are on the same level as the performance is for a 2-litre. As I could not keep the car for very long, and there was no time to take it to Monza or Modena track, it was important to select

roads on which it would really show its paces. So I decided to have a good run on the Torino-Ivrea Autostrada – the 'Tester's Paradise' as I call it – where the performance figures were taken on Fiat's accurately measured bases and then take it to the mountains surrounding Turin where I know a road almost entirely free from traffic which is an almost continuous sequence of curves, fast and slower, many of them offering perfect visibility so that you can drive practically as if you were on a race course.

Strangely, the car feels less quick off the mark than the stopwatch proves it to be, which is probably due to the entire absence of drama when a fast start is attempted: the clutch is not difficult at all and does not mind being engaged progressively to keep the revs in the useful torque curve, which is how to get the best results, for even on a damp track *wheelspin is killed by the rear weight bias and the big Michelin X 185 VR 14 tyres, mounted on 6½in wide rims (the light alloy wheels are from the Fiat Dino). Despite the remote and transverse position of the close-ratio five-speed gearbox, the gear change is beautifully smooth and quick. Fifth gear must be engaged just before the end of the kilometre, at about 118mph if the red line at 8,000rpm is not to be exceeded.*

125mph is reached very quickly – about 34 seconds – acceleration falling off noticeably only above 130mph when in the typical manner of an aerodynamically well designed car, speed continues to rise slowly until the real maximum is reached at 7,500 rpm. At this point, it takes just a breath of wind or a jolt from the road to raise the parked windscreen wiper blades a full five inches off the screen.

Stability at speed is wonderful and the car behaved beautifully in my favourite 125mph + S-bend of the Autostrada where it drifted through needing practically no correction at all. Unfortunately, I could not find out just how fast it could be taken with the Dino, as a shower of rain intervened after I had had only one clear run. Even in the wet, though, the car is extremely stable, but when it eventually goes, it goes quickly because of the very low polar moment of inertia so correction must be immediate and accurate.

An engine breathing down one's neck

Noise is an altogether different problem. With the engine literally breathing down one's neck, the Dino is by no means a silent car, though a short ride in a brand new one with a Ferrari tester in Modena showed that this – the 85th Dino to be made – was slightly better on this score than the first car off the line. The noise is mainly mechanical and no amount of sound proofing material will ever be able to conceal the fact that a twin-cam engine revving at 8,000rpm driving a five-speed box through a set of three transfer gears is only a matter of inches away from one's ears. Whether this noise (about the same as in a Porsche 911 I was using only a few days before when accelerating, but louder at a steady cruising speed) is really objectionable or not, must be up to the user. Some will find it unbearable and some others will find it a beautiful music. Sergio Pininfarina has no radio fitted and just listens to the engine. He tells me he usually drives with his side window slightly open because in this way the exhaust is better heard – and this is real music. Wind noise, on the other hand is practically non-existent, a result of the car's excellent aerodynamics and current production cars may be even better, for Sergio's car has two non-standard items: the front quarter windows have been deleted, which improves the lines but seriously reduces the stiffness of the window frame, and it has plastic covers over the headlights. These in fact are optional and though they improve the looks, tests have revealed that they add no more than 1kph in maximum speed.

Though the Dino is obviously a car for the open road, it certainly is best fun of all on the sort of semi-fast winding roads with good visibility where its superb agility can be fully exploited. In such surroundings, I know only very few cars which can compare with it for sheer pleasure of driving: the Lotus Elan is perhaps one of them and the Fiat 124 Spyder comes near it but lacks the power to catapult the car out of the bend. The Dino has about everything you could wish for in the circumstances: enormous cornering power, perfect balance which keeps the car in an almost perfectly neutral attitude whatever you do with the accelerator (as long as you don't provoke a power slide), and enough power to push you around into the following straight. However fast you corner, roll is hardly noticeable at all. The three twin-choke Weber carburettors however, were not designed to withstand the high cornering acceleration in the direction of the transverse engine, and there is occasionally a slight hesitation when the accelerator is depressed in these circumstances, which is not very welcome when the throttle is used as a means of controlling a drift. Fuel injection would, of course, cure this.

Though this is the only Ferrari-made car which has rack-and-pinion steering, it has, rather surprisingly, the slightly dead feel of all Ferrari steerings. Efficient damping is probably the reason, for there is practically no kick-back and the response is very positive and accurate. I was rather disturbed, however, by the fact that the action became considerably stiffer every half turn of the wheel — obviously caused by the upper universal joint in the steering column working at a rather sharp angle. On this score too, the latest cars have been improved, the upper part of the steering column being slightly more raked and shortened, to reduce the angle between it and the lower part. Manoeuvring the latest car in the grounds of a huge Agip service station showed the improvement to be considerable: some stiffness at 90 and 270 degrees either side of the straight ahead position could still be felt, but it is doubtful if it would be noticed in the normal course of driving to someone not actually watching for it.

For me, the servo-operated brakes were rather over-sensitive at speeds below 50 or 60mph. Above this, they were superb, but after I had driven as fast as reasonably possible on the winding roads of the mountains around Turin and had finally come down from Superga to Po level, some fade had become noticeable: retardation left little to be desired, but called for a harder push on the pedal.

Surprisingly good were the suspension and the insulation from road noise for which the huge 'pavés' of many of Turin's streets are a very exacting testing ground. The subdued road noise is particularly commendable in view of the big radial tyres and the crisp reactions of the car which suggest that all rubber joints in the suspension have been kept as hard as possible. It's a tribute to the rigidity of the structure. The reasonably soft springs are very efficiently damped and out on the highway, the car is very comfortable, with practically no trace of pitching, in spite of the comparatively short wheelbase. Even in town, the ride is not harsh and in these conditions, one appreciates the excellent visibility all round. Though real power comes in only around 5,000rpm the engine readily accepts city driving, accelerating smoothly from about 2,500rpm which with the smooth clutch and five-speed box makes easy work of traffic. To prevent plug fouling on cars being driven mainly in town, the same transistorized capacity ignition system, called 'Dinoplex' and made by Marelli is used as on the Fiat Dino. In case of failure of this system, a switch makes it possible to revert immediately to the normal ignition system.

Part of the charm of the Dino is its extremely pleasant and well proportioned body. The design is, of course, the work of Pininfarina who also made the first three prototypes, but the production cars are made by Scaglietti, in Modena, who work to the very exacting Pininfarina standards and really make a fine job of the car. One car is produced every working day. Accessibility to the engine by the forward rear deck panel is a strong point, though such units which may call for some service as the air filter, the carburettors, the distributor and three of the six plugs are all on the top part of the engine. The other three plugs are accessible only through a panel from inside the car. The driving position is superb, with well arranged pedals and a foot rest to the left of the clutch, and there is a wide range of adjustment for the seats which will go back far enough to make a really tall driver comfortable . The seats themselves are very well shaped and are also adjustable for rake, the whole seat tilting backwards. Though the spare wheel fairly fills the 'nose', there is quite a decent luggage boot behind the engine

An impressive sight — a brace of 246GTS's in pristine condition.

compartment. Inside the car, small items will find places in various lockers and shelves and even with the seats right back on their slides, there is room for larger things, like photo cameras, behind the seats, thanks to the slope of the squab. Heating and ventilation seem to be quite adequate and are certainly quickly mastered, with only two levers and a separate blower switch to work them.

The fuel consumption, I had no chance to check, but Sergio tells me it averages about 18 to 19mpg for fairly fast driving.

The car is now back in his hands, unfortunately, for by the time I handed it back to him, in his magnificent factory, in Grugliasco, a suburb of Turin, I had also decided that what I had thought to be noise was really beautiful music.

Paul Frère

EVOLUTIONARY PRESSURES

But buried within the praise which the 206 Dino attracted were comments and criticisms which spelt out the need for an improved version of the car. The lack of pull below 5,000rpm and the precarious parity with the contemporary Porsche 911 did not escape notice. The Dino badly needed a bigger engine with more torque at low rpm as well as more power.

As described in chapter 2, it got this engine in November 1969, ten months after Paul Frère had reported on his day with the 206. By that time Fiat had acquired their interest in Ferrari, which soon changed its character. The pace of development and production rapidly quickened, and the new 246 Dino with its 2.4-litre iron-block engine was launched with the intention of producing it in substantial numbers (by Ferrari standards) and in the knowledge that serious efforts to sell it would be necessary. That meant a new era of changed attitudes in which road-test

cars were regarded, albeit with many misgivings, as a necessary evil.

As a result, 246 Dinos were available for Paul Frère and others to drive as early as the January of 1970, and two months afterwards a right-hand drive model was made available in Britain for *Motor* by the UK importers, Maranello concessionnaires, for a brief group appraisal in conjunction with other Ferrari models. Just over a year later, a 246 was offered to *Motor* for a full road-test, which is reproduced here.

ROAD TEST
Reproduced from *Motor* 10 July 1971

Ferrari Dino 246GT

Perfection is an absolute quality found only in nature or that part of it we call genius: it is rarely applicable to the collection of compromises known as the motor car. Occasionally, however, we do test cars that closely approach perfection, missing it only in details of execution or performance. Into this rare category comes the 2.4-litre transverse mid-engined Ferrari Dino 246GT.

It attains this elevated classification not only because its designers and stylists have got virtually all their sums right — it cannot be faulted in any area of importance — but because they have endowed it with two additional virtues. The first is beauty — at least in the eyes of everyone at Motor *who beheld it. The second is the car's forgiving and controllable behaviour when its limit of adhesion is finally exceeded, an important advance for a mid-engined vehicle which has revived our wavering faith in the concept for road-going cars. But few drivers will ever manage to lose the Dino, for it has the tremendous grip characteristic of this configuration. Unlike some other mid-engined cars, however, it has adequate* threequarter rear visibility (excellent everywhere else) and a boot which is as capacious as the airy cockpit. Such spaciousness follows from an overall length almost as great as that of the latest Ford Cortina, yet with an overall height of only 45in. Pininfarina's graceful styling contrives to make it look a tiny jewel of a car, as minuscule as is claimed in the sales literature.

Then there is the superb engine, the equally superb gearbox, the exceptionally comfortable ride, the excellent driving position and the well laid out controls. Perhaps the Dino's only significant fault is its fuel consumption, which is rather heavy for its performance; apart from this we had no more than one or two minor complaints about such matters as ventilation and the location of the instruments. Nor is the Dino an unattainable dream: you have to be rich to own one but you needn't be a millionaire, for it is the 'cheap' Ferrari, costing only £5,486 in Britain — it has been available in rhd form since October. At this price demand should greatly exceed supply and the car constitutes formidable opposition to the Porsche 911S.

Performance and economy

The original transverse-engined Ferrari Dino announced at the 1967 Turin Show was powered by a 2-litre light alloy 65° V6 with four chain-driven overhead camshafts built by Fiat to a Ferrari design for the Dinos of both companies. Two years later this engine was replaced by another of the same configuration but with a cast-iron block and capacity increased to 2.4 litres; it is now built — again for both Dinos — by Ferrari at Maranello. For the Ferrari Dino it develops 195 (net) bhp — 15bhp more than does the Fiat Dino version — at no less than 7600rpm, and 165.5lb ft of torque at 5500rpm.

Ignoring the choke lever between the seats we found that it always started easily from cold, as is usual with Weber carburetters (of which there are three) by simply depressing the throttle pedal a few times to make the accelerator pumps squirt neat petrol into the cylinders. Once started it idled easily and pulled without hesitation at once. To produce nearly 200bhp from 2.4 litres the Ferrari engine has to be very highly tuned by production standards, yet it pulls extraordinarily well from low speeds. For demonstration purposes it can be made to do so from 1000rpm in fifth by carefully feeding in the throttle, though if the pedal is floored at around 1500rpm the engine will hesitate, maybe die. But from 1800rpm onwards the engine pulls with real vigour, gathering particular strength at just under 3500rpm and continuing to deliver a surge of power right up to the 7800rpm limit — surely the highest of any car currently in series production. And throughout this rev range the engine is utterly smooth and unfussed, so much so that care must be exercised to prevent over-revving. All this to the accompaniment of a mellow baying from the four exhaust pipes combined with a whine from the camshaft chains and a faint excited gnashing from the valvegear. Everyone liked this exciting noise, but a few of our test staff thought it just a little too loud and found it tiring on long journeys, even though it reduces to a contented burble when cruising at 100–110mph, at which speed there is very little wind noise provided the doors are properly shut — they need a good slam.

Despite the handicap of considerable weight for a sports car — 23.3cwt. unladen — and by absolute standards relatively modest capacity and power, the Dino is a very quick car. It gets to 60mph from rest in 7.1 sec., to 100mph in 17.6 sec. and will comfortably pull maximum revs in top gear giving a maximum speed of 148mph. The engine is so torquey that this gear often feels lower than it actually is, inducing an initial underestimation of speed. The Dino's excellent performance in the upper part of the speed range follows largely from its excellent aerodynamics as demonstrated by its flat fuel consumption curve which remains comfortably above 20mpg at 100mph. The

The dramatic, curvaceous lines of the
Dino 246 (above) still command
admiration more than twenty years
after the car's launch.

The view of the Dino 246 (below) most
likely to be encountered by other, less
fortunate motorists!

shape also has other important aerodynamic qualities, for the car feels impressively secure and stable at very high speeds and proved to be virtually impervious to side winds.

Unfortunately the low drag factor does not seem to have counterbalanced the disadvantage of considerable weight — and perhaps of rich-running Webers — for the fuel consumption is rather poor and once or twice plunged below 15mpg during particularly fast runs, though the final overall figure was 16.1mpg of 5-star fuel. But owners will probably find, as we did, that after the novelty of the Dino's high performance has worn off, it is possible to get along almost as quickly as before with rather less use of the revs and gears; the fuel consumption then improves to the 17–19mpg level, giving a range from the 15.5 gallon tank of around 260 miles.

Transmission

Following the Ferrari tradition there is a gate at the base of the Dino's floor-mounted gearlever to define the positions of the five speeds which are arranged Porsche-fashion: first and reverse are to the left of the upper four gears laid out in the usual H. No spring loading is used except for reverse, obtained with a downward push. At a casual glance the presence of the gate might seem to introduce navigational inhibitions, and indeed our testers did need a little practice to get used to the change from first to second. But after a time the presence of the gate is forgotten and the first-second movement becomes as easy and natural — though perhaps a little slower — as, right from the start, do the movements between all the other gears. The gearbox then reveals itself as being superb with unobtrusive but effective synchromesh which allows lightning changes to be sliced through. The lightness and feeling of precision is remarkable in view of the distant location of the transmission behind and beneath the engine to which it is coupled by three spur gears.

On our test car, the quicker the changes the more easily they went through, as the rather heavy clutch did not always disengage completely when depressed slowly. Like the throttle, however, it was very progressive in action so smooth changes are easy once the driver has allowed for the fact that although the engine revs rise quickly enough when the throttle is blipped, they tend to die slowly, perhaps because of a heavy flywheel.

Well-spaced maxima of 41mph, 59mph, 81mph and 110mph are possible in the four indirect gears. The engine's excellent torque at low revs made it rarely necessary to use bottom gear for anything other than starting off. Only in fourth was some transmission whine audible.

Handling and brakes

When it comes to getting round corners the Ferrari Dino has all the advantages – and makes use of them. One such is racing-style double-wishbone suspension at both ends. Another is the location of the engine just behind the driver which puts more weight on the rear wheels for good traction in slippery conditions and less on the front wheels to allow the use of fat tyres with direct manual steering. Both these last two ends have in particular been admirably achieved on the Ferrari: it has monster 205 XVR Michelin radials guided at the front by superbly precise, direct steering which gives good feel with little kickback and is one of the joys of the car.

The inevitable result of all this is an ability to go round corners, which makes ordinary cars seem wholly inadequate. Only when trying a normal saloon after the Dino does a driver realize just how effortlessly and quickly he has been going. Terms like understeer and oversteer are generally pretty academic: the car just steers. Further acquaintance reveals that taking a corner under power tends to create not so much gentle oversteer as a useful tightening of the line.

So much for impressions on the road – we needed the relative security of a closed test track to learn more about the Dino's phenomenally high limits. Unlike many mid-engined cars it does not always understeer with power, and oversteer without it. On fast bends the gentle oversteer tendency was confirmed; on slow bends we were able to make the front end plough outwards with power. Equally, a vicious bootful of throttle in second could break the tail away though in an easily catchable way.

But there is a much more important question to be answered. Even the Dino must run out of grip eventually – what happens when it does? For the practised anticipation and lightning responses of the professional racing driver, mid-engined cars may be fine, but with their centrally located masses they do tend to spin rapidly when all is finally lost, an unsatisfactory characteristic for the more ordinary mortals likely to drive Dinos on the road, one that has made us hesitate to endorse the concept for practical roadgoing sports cars.

Such hesitations are swept aside by the forgiving nature of the Dino. Helped by a limited-slip differential, it retains a large measure of its traction and cornering power in the wet, though it does have one vice: a tendency to plane outwards at the front on puddles and rivulets perhaps a little more than would a front-engined car. But if you lift your foot sharply off the accelerator in a corner the car responds with nothing more than a slight twitch that calls for little steering correction. Even if this is done when cornering nearly on the limit, the tail breaks away in a gentle and controllable way, a response to which we had reason to feel gratitude as fuel surge tended to make our test car cut out when entering a corner under the combination of deceleration and turning. It is this safe

Motor road test No. 30/71   Dino Ferrari 246GT

Make: *Ferrari. Model: Dino 246GT.* **Makers:** *Ferrari Automobili S.p.A. SEFAC, casella postale 589, 41100 Modena, Italy.* **Concessionaires:** *Maranello Concession-* *aires Ltd, Egham-by-pass, Surrey.* **Price:** *£4,200 plus £1,285.63 purchase tax equals £5,485.63. Electric window lifters £83.55 extra with tax.*

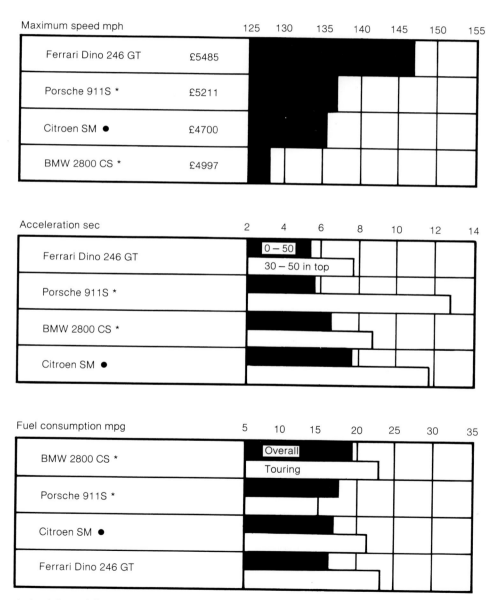

* obsolete models
● estimated

Performance tests carried out by *Motor*'s staff at the Motor Industry Research Association proving ground, Lindley.

Test Data: World copyright reserved; no unauthorised reproduction in whole or in part.

CONDITIONS
Weather: Warm and dry
Temperature: 64–68°F
Barometer: 29.85 in Hg
Surface: Dry concrete
Fuel: 101 octane (RM) 5-star rating

MAXIMUM SPEEDS

		mph	kph
Max. speed		148	238
4th gear		110	177
3rd gear	at 7,800	81	130
2nd gear	rpm	59	95
1st gear		41	66

ACCELERATION TIMES

mph	sec.
0–30	2.6
0–40	3.6
0–50	5.5
0–60	7.1
0–70	9.2
0–80	11.4
0–90	14.5
0–100	17.6
0–110	22.0
0–120	28.5
Standing quarter mile	15.4
Standing kilometre	27.8

mph	Top sec.	4th sec.	3rd sec.
10– 30	—	—	5.2
20– 40	8.4	6.0	3.6
30– 50	7.8	5.0	3.3
40– 60	7.8	4.5	3.6
50– 70	7.2	5.3	3.6
60– 80	7.3	5.4	4.1
70– 90	8.2	5.5	—
80–100	8.9	6.2	—
90–110	9.5	7.2	—
100–120	11.8	—	—

FUEL CONSUMPTION
Touring (consumption midway between 30 mph and maximum less 5% allowance for acceleration) — 23.0 mpg
Overall — 16.1 mpg
(=17.5 litres/100km)
Total test distance — 1,294 miles

BRAKES
Pedal pressure, deceleration and equivalent stopping distance from 30 mph.

lb.	g.	ft.
25	0.34	88
50	0.71	42
75	0.86	35
100	0.92	33
135	0.98	31
Handbrake	0.31	97

FADE TEST
20 stops at ½g deceleration at 1 min. intervals from a speed midway between 40 mph and maximum speed (=95.5 mph)

	lb.
Pedal force at beginning	35
Pedal force at 10th stop	35
Pedal force at 20th stop	35

STEERING

	ft.
Turning circle between kerbs:	
Left	37
Right	36
Turns of steering wheel from lock to lock	3.1
Steering wheel deflection for 50ft diameter circle	1.25 turns

CLUTCH
Free pedal movement = ½in.
Additional movement to disengage clutch completely = 2½in.
Maximum pedal load = 43lb.

SPEEDOMETER

Indicated	10	20	30	40	50	60	70
True	10	19	27	37½	47½	57½	67½

Indicated		80	90	100
True		77	87	97

Distance recorder 3% fast.

WEIGHT

Kerb weight (unladen with fuel for approximately 50 miles)	23.3 cwt.
Front/rear distribution	43/57
Weight laden as tested	27.1 cwt.

behaviour in extreme conditions that makes the Dino so outstanding.

To match this handling are brakes of equal calibre. The four huge outboard ventilated discs are operated with servo assistance through a front/rear split hydraulic system. Surprisingly, in view of the 43/57 front/rear weight distribution, there is a pressure relief valve in the rear line, showing how much weight can be transferred to the front wheels during heavy braking. In mid-engined cars this may not be enough to prevent front wheel lock up under heavy braking — especially in the wet — but of this vice the Dino was completely free. Though the pressures required were rather higher than is usual nowadays — the maximum 1g deceleration being achieved with a force of 135lb — the brakes felt immensely progressive and reassuring in their action. As might be expected from their racing heritage, they did not fade either on the road or during our test, nor were they affected by a thorough soaking in the watersplash. But a really strenuous pull on the handbrake gave a deceleration of no more than 0.31g.

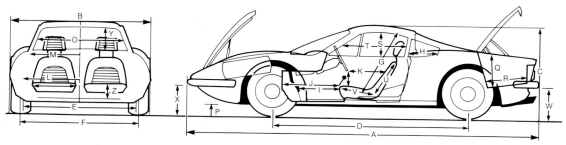

		ft	in			ft	in			ft	in			ft	in
A	overall length	13	10.75	J	legroom			O	windscreen			U	seat back		
B	overall width	5	7		max.	2	6		width	3	4		height	1	7.5
C	unladen height	3	9		min.	2	1.25	P	min. ground			V	seat base		
D	wheelbase	7	8.25	K	seat to steering				clearance		5.5		depth	1	6.5
E	front track	4	7.75		wheel	1	11	Q	boot height	1	6.25	W	rear bumper		
F	rear track	4	8.75	L	front elbow			R	boot depth	1	6		height	1	3.5
G	com. seat to roof.	3	0.5		width	4	6.5	S	side window			X	front bumper		
H	rear quarter			M	front shoulder				height	1	0.25		height	1	2.5
	light	1	2.25		width	4	0	T	side window			Y	windscreen		
I	pedal to seat			N	seat width	1	8.25		length	2	5.5		height	2	5
	max.	1	10.5									Z	seat height		6.25
	min.	1	6.25												

ENGINE

Block material	Cast iron
Head material	Light alloy
Cylinders	6 in V
Cooling system	water
Bore and stroke	92.5mm (3.64in)
	60mm (2.36in)
Cubic capacity	2418 cc (148.1 cu.in)
Main bearings	4
Valves	Dohc
Compression ratio	9.0:1
Carburettors	Three Weber 40DCN F/7
Fuel pumps	Two Bendix electric
Oil Filter	Full flow
Max. power (net)	195 bhp at 7600 rpm
Max. torque (net)	165-5lb.ft. at
	5500 rpm

TRANSMISSION

Clutch sdp diaphragm mechanically operated

Internal gearbox ratios

Top gear	0.857:1
4th gear	1.125:1
3rd gear	1.524:1
2nd gear	2.117:1
1st gear	3.075:1
Reverse	2.667:1
Synchromesh	All forward ratios
Final drive	4.44:1 spur transfer gears

Mph at 1,000 r.p.m. in:

Top gear	19.0
4th gear	14.1
3rd gear	10.4
2nd gear	7.5
1st gear	5.2

CHASSIS AND BODY

Construction   Steel tubular and sheet construction.

BRAKES

Type   Servo assisted ventilated discs operated by split hydraulic system with pressure relief valve in rear line.
Dimensions 10.6in dia.   front and rear

SUSPENSION AND STEERING

Front	Independent by wishbones with coil springs and an anti-roll bar
Rear	Independent by wishbones with coil springs and an anti-roll bar

Shock absorbers:
Front }
Rear }   Telescopic, double-acting Konis

Steering type	Cam gears rack and pinion
Tyres	205/70VR 14X Michelin
Wheels	14in.
Rim size	6½ in.

COACHWORK AND EQUIPMENT

Starting handle	No
Tool kit contents	Reflective triangle, jack, brace, pliers, Philips and ordinary screwdrivers, plug, carburetter and open-ended spanners
Jack	Screw pillar
Jacking points	One each side
Battery 12 volt	negative earth 60 amp hrs capacity
Number of electrical fuses	12
Headlamps	Halogen type
Indicators	Self-cancelling flashers
Reversing lamps	Yes
Screen wipers	Electric, self parking variable speed
Screen washers	Electric
Sun visors	Two

Locks:	
With ignition key	Doors
Interior heater	Fresh air
Upholstery:	
Floor covering	Carpets
Alternative body styles	None
Major extras available	Electric window lifters

MAINTENANCE

Fuel tank capacity	15.5 galls
Sump	12 pints SAE 10W30
Gearbox and final drive	8 pints SAE EP80
Steering gear	035 Shell Spirax EP90
Coolant	30 (2 drain taps)
Chassis lubrication	Every 3000 miles to 4 points
Maximum service interval	3000 miles
Ignition timing	6° btdc
Contact breaker gap	0.012−0.015in.
Sparking plug gap	0.16−0.20 in.
Sparking plug type	Champion N60Y
Tappet clearance (cold)	Inlet 0.007in. Exhaust 0.017in.

Valve timing:

inlet opens	40° btdc
inlet closes	52° abdc
exhaust opens	53° bbdc
exhaust closes	31° atdc
Rear wheel toe-in	1/16 −1/8in.
Rear wheel camber	0° 50′ ± 1° 15′
Front wheel toe-in	1/16 −1/8in.
Camber angle	0° + 15′
Castor angle	4°
King pin inclination	9° 3′

Tyre pressures:

Front	27 psi
Rear	31 psi

Comfort and controls

Few saloon cars other than Citroens − let alone sports cars − ride better than the Dino. Firm, rather than harsh at low speeds, the suspension simply smothers the biggest bumps and soaks up undulations without pitch, float or bottoming. The comfort provided contributes greatly to the feeling of security so characteristic of the car. Unfortunately, the ride is not matched by the seats, which could only suit midgets and have rolls across the tops of their backrests which dug into the shoulder blades of even our shortest drivers. These backrests incorporate adjustable headrests but do not recline − there wouldn't be room for them to do so anyway. In partial compensation for these defects the range of fore-and-aft adjustment is enough to satisfy the legroom requirements of human beings at the other extreme of size as represented by our resident 6ft 5in giant. And the seats do provide good lateral support, helped by the rest for the left foot which constitutes an excellent bracing spot.

Sports cars tend to have cramped cockpits; Italian cars to have the steering wheel too far away and the pedals too close. Though the Dino is both sporting and Italian, its small steering wheel (which has a leather-covered rim) and its pedals are so well located that everyone was able to achieve a comfortable driving position, regardless of size. Gearlever and handbrake, too, could be reached without effort by all our test staff when wearing seatbelts. Fingertip control over all the services completes the feeling of unity with the machine that the Dino imparts. On the left there is an indicator stalk with behind it a longer stalk controlling all the modes of side and headlamp operation, while in conformity with another of our preferences the horn is operated by a button at the centre of the wheel. A right-hand stalk controls the washers and the wipers which have no intermittent action but can be varied in speed by a rheostat mounted on the facia near the stalk. The wiper arms have an overlapping 'clap hands' action which allows them to clear the screen close to both edges, though the wiped area should extend further up the screen for tall drivers. These arms also accelerate as they move from their central positions and even at their lowest speeds make a loud and wearing thump as they contact the frame at the sides of the windscreen. At medium to fast speeds they flick over the frame completely and can be seen through the quarterlights.

The deep, wide and steeply raked screen gives excellent forward visibility over the low bonnet. This falls away towards the ground between the wheelarches out of the driver's sight so that there is more car in front than is at first realized, calling for extra care during parking manoeuvres. In contrast the blunt Kamm-type tail is easily seen from the cockpit. It is seen through the rear window which is one of the Dino's most striking features; nearly vertical and no more than 8in high, it curls backwards through 90° at each end to meet the rear quarterlights set into the flanks of the car. In this way it provides a fair measure of the important three-quarter rear vision so lacking in some mid-engined designs while helping to isolate the occupants from engine noise, and in its protected location at the forward end of the rear deck, remains virtually untouched by dirt or rain. At night the halogen headlamps were good both when dipped and when on main beam so long as their plastic covers were kept clean.

There is virtually no wind noise below 100mph − it builds up gradually thereafter. Road noise is moderate despite the tautness of the steering and suspension which suggests minimum compliance. Radial tyres notwithstanding, it is more high-frequency roar than low-frequency thump.

Hot and cold air is admitted into the interior through four swivelling 'egg-slicer' vents, two in the footwells and two on the facia, close to the screen but a long way from the occupants. These are controlled by

A steeply-raked screen means a high heat input in summer and causes the standard facia trim-cloth to fade quickly.

independent distribution levers for each side of the car which flank a central temperature control lever. This is progressive in action but without the two booster fans (one for the footwells and one for the screen) the throughput is small. With the heater shut off, the screen booster provided just enough cool air in town for the warmish days of our test, and the volume can be increased without introducing much extra noise at speed by winding the side windows down a little.

Fittings and furniture

Betraying a desire to match the graceful exterior and the curved plan-form of the windscreen — which is delineated by the deep shelf of the facia — the stylists have given the cowled instrument cluster an elliptical shape. Like the facia it is covered with a black velvety material. Neither the shape nor the material were popular with our staff despite their functional attributes in minimising obstruction to the base of the screen and in eliminating unwanted reflections. Less popular still were the locations of the speedometer and rev counter towards the ends of the major axis of their elliptical enclosure, just where they are dangerously obscured by the wheel rim to all but very short drivers — dangerous because the engine is so smooth that even its very high 7800rpm limit could easily be exceeded. At no time did it show the slightest signs of rising temperature or falling oil pressure, yet the relevant gauges have been

given pride of place, right in front of the driver.

Also covered in the velvety material, and retained by a cheap-looking catch but no lock, is the lid of the moderate-sized glove compartment. Together with the boxes built in to the doors this provides most of the oddments space, though there is room for small packets, newspapers and the like behind the seats. A vanity mirror in the passenger's sun visor, an ashtray and a cigarette lighter complete the cockpit fittings. The front compartment is filled by the spare wheel and toolkit, but the conventional rear

A thoroughly desirable pairing (left): in the foreground a perfectly preserved Dino 246 GT; alongside, a sleek 1970 Ferrari Daytona 365 Cabriolet.

boot is large for a sports car, taking 5.6 cu ft of our Revelation suitcases.

The Dino is very well equipped electrically. It has, for example, reversing lights, red warning lights in the door edges and lights for all three compartments. In the front compartment there are boxes of fuses each of which is clearly marked in three languages with the services it protects, while in the boot at the rear is the transitorised ignition system with its spare coil. Our test car was additionally fitted with the optional (£83.55 extra) electric window lifters.

Servicing and accessibility

When an engine is located in the centre of a car it is not easy to get at. The Ferrari's unit is not too bad in this respect except for the long dipstick which requires careful *threading into its tube in the forward bank of cylinders under the hinged engine cover. Even minor repairs, however — like replacing blown exhaust gaskets — could prove expensive as the bulkhead in front of the engine cannot be removed so the complete engine/transmission unit may have to be removed for attention of this sort, though it is accessible through a removable panel at the rear of the boot and through detachable panels in the wheelarches.*

Servicing, which includes some chassis greasing, is required every 3000 miles and there are 7 Ferrari dealers and distributors in the UK. There is a good toolkit which includes a reflective triangle, and an informative and well-illustrated three-language handbook. We found the pillar jack rather stiff in its action.

THE DINO TODAY

The question most often asked about any classic is how well it compares with the equivalent cars of today, and it is a question which is seldom easy to answer in a simple and unequivocal way. For the Dino a considered reply is in any case complicated by the existence of two different models: the early — and rare — 206 and the later 246 produced in far greater numbers. Let us begin by considering first the better-known Dino 246, returning later to the 206 to summarise any differences.

PERFORMANCE AND ECONOMY

Only in straight-line performance is it possible to give a reasonably clear-cut answer to the how-does-it-compare question: with a 0–60mph (96.5kph) acceleration time of 7.1sec and a top speed of 148mph (238kph) (according to *Motor*) the 246GT Dino is still a very quick car indeed. Agreed, this performance looks feeble against the rocket-like acceleration (below 5sec to 60mph (96.5kph)) and flying top speeds (170–200mph (273–322kph)) of modern supercars like the Ferrari F40 and the Porsche 959. But then the Dino was always designed as a 'junior league' supercar with a lower power/weight ratio than the fastest contemporary cars such as V12 Ferraris. And even though the average car of the late eighties is very much faster than the average car of the early seventies, the Dino has not been outclassed in performance by more ordinary cars. While the best 'hot hatches' of today, for instance, may have similar 0–60mph (96.5kph) acceleration times, their maximum speeds are generally in the 120–130mph (193–209kph) range.

Moreover, it's not just what a car does that matters, but the way it does it, and in this the Dino has few rivals, past or present. Take the gearchange, for instance. Most drivers need a little time to get used to the exposed Ferrari gate, the dog-leg first-second change, and to the reluctance of second gear to engage for the first couple of miles after a cold start until the transmission oil has warmed up. But after familiarisation, lightning up or down changes become possible: shifts can be made, with negligible obstruction, as quickly as the hand and foot can be moved.

Then there's the marvellous music of the engine, a typical Ferrari sound, compounded of a rich exhaust burble, a whine of the timing chains and an excited gnashing of the valvegear.

On a more objective level, the performance of the 246 is still not disgraced by comparison with equivalent cars of the late eighties such as the Ferrari 328, the Porsche 911 Carrera Sport and the Lotus Esprit Turbo*, as the following comparison shows:

* 1988 model

	Dino 246	Ferrari 328	Porsche 911	Lotus Esprit Turbo
Capacity, cc	2,418	3,185	3,164	2,174
Power, bhp/rpm	195/7,600	270/7,000	231/5,900	215/6,000
Torque, lb ft/rpm	166/5,500	224/5,500	209/4,800	220/4,250
30–50 mph in 5th, sec	7.8	7.0	7.6	9.6
0–60 mph, sec	7.1	5.5	5.3	5.4
0–100 mph, sec	17.6	13.8	13.6	13.3
Top speed, mph	148	158.5	151.1	150
kph	238	255	243	241
Overall fuel consumpt, mpg	16.1	18.9	21.1	19.6
litre/100 km	17.5	14.9	13.4	14.4
Mph/1,000 rpm in top	19.0	21.0	24.3	23.7
Unladen weight* cwt	23.3	26.1	23.0	27.3
kg	1,186	1,325	1,166	1,386

* With fuel for approx 50 miles

(Sources: 246 Dino, *Motor* 10/7/71; Ferrari 328, *Motor* 21/6/86; Porsche 911 Carrera Sport, *Motor* 22/10/83; Lotus Esprit Turbo HC, *Autocar* 20/4/88.)

There are two areas in which the performance of the 246 Dino is now clearly outclassed. The first is in its 0–60mph (96.5kph) acceleration time which is some two seconds slower than a typical time for equivalent modern cars. Obtaining these figures calls for a brutal technique – which no sensible owner would subject his or her car to – involving much spinning of the rear wheels and clutch-dropping at high rpm, but it does create a standard basis of comparison in which outright power, mid-range torque, gearing and ease of gearchanging all play a part.

More significant, though, are the improvements in power, torque and efficiency that have become commonplace during the past two decades. All the modern engines equivalent to the Dino's are much more powerful and develop more torque at the same or lower rpm, *yet despite being greater in capacity give far better fuel consumption.* The 16.1mpg overall fuel consumption obtained by *Motor*'s hard-driving testers back in 1971 simply wouldn't be acceptable today (only the inefficient rotary-engined Mazda RX7 remains at this level) and compares very badly with, for example, the 21.1mpg obtained in 1983 from the Porsche 911 Carrera Sport. For two of the cars considered here – the Ferrari 328 and the Lotus Esprit Turbo – the improvement in efficiency may partly be due to the incorporation of a long-established design feature that Ferrari could well have adopted for the Dino had they chosen: four-valve combustion chambers. (The Ford Escort RS1600, remember, was introduced in 1971.) But for the much better fuel consumption in relation to performance routinely available today, we mostly have to thank a steady series of subtle improvements in combustion quality, fuel metering (usually by injection) ignition performance and electronic engine management.

Interestingly, on the other hand, the current sportscars in this comparison are not significantly lighter than the Dino, yet the structures of racing cars have become vastly more sophisticated than in the early seventies and we are constantly hearing of new lightweight materials being adopted for motor vehicles.

The turbocharger fitted to the Lotus represents another major trend which has developed since the Dino was launched. The ability of the Lotus engine to develop a competitive power output despite a capacity disadvantage of 1,000cc demonstrates the value of the turbo; the poor 30–50mph (48–80kph) acceleration time in fifth demonstrates its weakness.

ROADHOLDING AND HANDLING

A proper assessment of the Dino's roadholding and handling would call for a group of competitive ancient and modern cars, some experienced road-testers to drive them and preferably a circuit closed to the public on which limits of adhesion could safely be explored – an expensive exercise to set up. All the evidence suggests, however, that the Dino's outright cornering power is only slightly lower than that of equivalent modern mid-engined cars and that its handling remains rather better.

Consider the outright cornering power. This depends upon many factors, but the most important are a low weight, a low centre of gravity, a wide track, fat tyres and good suspension geometry. In all these respects the Dino still scores well, as can be seen if it is again compared with a Ferrari 328, a Porsche 911 Carrera Sport and a Lotus Esprit Turbo:

	Dino 246	Ferrari 328	Porsche 911	Lotus Esprit Turbo
Overall height, in	45.0	44.4	52.0	45.8
Overall width, in	67.0	68.1	65.0	73.2
Track, front/rear, in	55.3/56.8	58.3/57.5	56.3/59	60.0/61.2
Tyres front/rear	205/70– 205/70	205/55– 225/50	205/55– 225/50	195/60– 235/60

The unmistakable prancing horse of Ferrari (left) *and the discreet name badge* (right) *which adorns the rear of the 246GT.*

As already mentioned, the Dino is about the same weight as its modern equivalents, and as the above table shows, it is still one of the lowest cars ever built, with a proportionately low centre of gravity. Similarly, while much has been learned about bump-steer, compliance-steer and other subtleties of suspension geometry, the basic characteristics of a double-wishbone set-up were as well understood in the late sixties when the Dino was designed as they are today, so again, the 246 has little to fear in this particular aspect of design.

In addition, the mean tyre widths of the modern rivals are only slightly greater than the Dino's. But the lower profile of these modern tyres will give them greater cornering power, and the Dino is significantly narrower in track than the other cars, especially the Lotus. These factors are bound to add up to a slightly higher outright cornering power at a steady speed in a curve of constant radius.

But whereas the handling of ordinary family saloons has improved immensely in the last twenty years, the handling of high-performance mid-engined cars has not climbed much above the level reached when the Dino was introduced. For example, in their road-test yearbook of 1989, *Autocar &*

Motor describe the handling of the Lotus Esprit by saying: 'Like many mid-engined cars, the Esprit won't tolerate sloppy driving. Go deep into a corner on a trailing throttle or come off the brake too late and you'll need to be quick with the wheel to catch the tail'.

Compare this comment with the statements in *Motor*'s original road-test of 1971; 'But if you lift your foot sharply off the accelerator in a corner the car responds with nothing more than a slight twitch that calls for little correction. Even if this is done when cornering nearly on the limit, the tail breaks away in a gentle and controllable way, a response to which we had reason to feel gratitude as fuel surge tended to make our test car cut out when entering a corner due to the combination of deceleration and turning'. Four years after that test, in 1975, *Motor* again confirmed the forgiving nature of the Dino's handling in a comparative evaluation with a Porsche 911 Carrera.

Easing off in the middle of a corner is, of course, a poor driving technique, but in the crowded conditions of today the unexpected sometimes occurs despite the most careful anticipation and the best modern cars are highly tolerant of such circumstances — they're on your side in an emergency. The Dino is just such a car.

But this analysis of the subject wouldn't be complete without mentioning two more recent influences, the 'hot hatch syndrome' and the 'width factor'. In 1988 *Car* magazine proved to their own satisfaction what experienced road-testers had long suspected: that the best high-performance hatchbacks of today such as the Peugeot 205GTi or the Golf GTi combine excellent performance with such high standards of roadholding and handling that they can comfortably keep up with a hard-driven fast mid-engined car on twisty country roads, given two drivers of equal skill.

In such an exercise, moreover, quite a few modern mid-engined cars — the delightful little Fiat XI/9 excepted — are severely hampered by their excessive width. The Lotus Esprit used in *Car*'s comparison, for instance, is 6ft 1in (1.9m) wide (compared to 5ft 7in (1.67m) for the Dino) while the Ferrari Testarossa is a ridiculous 6ft 5¾in (1.98m) wide and the Lamborghini Countach an inch wider still — which makes them as broad in the beam as a small truck and wildly impractical for anything other than motorway driving. It simply isn't necessary for cars to be so wide. If matched against a modern hot hatch on the winding country roads of Britain, France or Italy, therefore, a Dino could well fare slightly better than some mid-engined cars of the late eighties.

COMFORT

High-performance sports cars are in general bought more for excitement and driving pleasure than comfort. Even the most dedicated enthusiast, however, can appreciate the fine distinction between an engine which is noisy rather than melodious, a suspension system which is harsh rather than firm, or accommodation which is cramped rather than snug.

In such matters the Dino again scores well. It cannot be considered quiet by the standards of today, but neither is it the sort of car that gives the occupants a headache after a long journey. Wind noise is low, and so — surprisingly, despite the evident lack of compliance in the suspension — is road noise. The major source of noise, is of course, the engine, but at 100–110mph (161–177kph) in top, a sensible motorway cruising pace in countries where such speeds are still legal, it settles back to a relatively muted hum against which a conversation can be maintained without too much strain.

But it is nevertheless in its combination of low overall gearing with an engine of relatively small capacity which runs to an exceptionally high speed that the Dino most shows its age. To squeeze adequate performance out of it, very high revs must be used. There's quite a lot more acceleration to come between, say, 6,500rpm — peak revs for most equivalent engines today — and the 7,600rpm maximum power speed. And with a fifth gear that gives only 19mph/1,000rpm, high-speed cruising is a good deal fussier than it need be. Although the Dino's successors the 308 and 328 retained rather low gearing, other manufacturers have demonstrated the benefits of higher overall gearing giving 24–26mph/1,000rpm in top in conjunction with a larger and more efficient modern engine. The result is more relaxed cruising at high speed and better fuel consumption at no significant sacrifice in acceleration through the gears.

In ride comfort, on the other hand, the Dino is in no way outdated. Highly praised in original road tests, the Dino's springing is stiff enough to keep roll angles low but soft enough to soak up bumps with efficiency. Modern mid-engined cars are little, if at all, better in this respect, even though the ride/handling compromise of the best saloons and hatchbacks has advanced amazingly during the past few years, the Peugeots 405, 205GTi and 309GTi being especially good.

With a comfortable driving position, sufficient legroom for all but the exceptionally tall, just enough space behind the seats for a slim briefcase and a rear boot big enough to take several suitcases, the

Dino is also a practical grand tourer. Its heating system is crude, though, and its ventilation non-existent — happily the car can be run with the windows open in hot weather without much wind noise or buffeting. (US versions of the car were available with air conditioning.) The backrests of the seats are too short, also, and the instruments are poorly sited, the speedometer and rev-counter being obscured by the steering wheel for drivers of a wide range of heights. At least one owner has rearranged the instruments of his car, placing the speedometer and rev-counter in the middle and the auxiliary dials at the ends of the display.

Most owners, though, have considered these minor defects to be far outweighed by the car's numerous virtues.

THE 206

In most respects the 206 is very similar to the 246, with one major exception: it is slightly slower, and its 2-litre engine which runs to 8,000rpm has to work even harder, making the car a little noisier and fussier.

With body panels of aluminium instead of steel, and aluminium, too, for the cylinder block in place of cast iron, the 206 might be thought to have a major weight advantage over its successor, the 246. Indeed the 206 is sometimes quoted as weighing no more than 2,000lb (909kg) or 17.9cwt, but such figures must have been taken from early prototypes, because production models weighed around 2,500lb (1,140kg) or 22.4cwt, only 1cwt or some 50kg lighter than the 246.

A brief analysis of the factors involved suggests reasons for the lack of difference. Both cars have a heavy chassis built up from a generous quantity of steel tube and plate, so the substitution of materials for the largely unstressed body panels may be expected to have relatively little influence on overall weight. Similarly, since the engines of both cars already had light alloy cylinder heads, plus at the same time an equal and very large number of heavy steel or cast iron parts — including four camshafts — the saving in weight which accrues from the use of an aluminium block is likely to be valuable but modest.

But the 1cwt (50kg) weight advantage of the 206, though small, helps to offset the smaller output of its engine. As already mentioned, this was claimed to be 180bhp by Ferrari, but thought by contemporary observers to be a little less in view of the 160bhp developed by the virtually identical Fiat version of the engine, though admittedly this latter power unit was designed to peak at a slightly lower speed — 7,200rpm instead of 8,000rpm. If the 180bhp is accepted, however, it gives the 206 virtually the same power/weight ratio as the 246 with its 195bhp engine, and this is confirmed by contemporary test values for the 0–60mph (0–96.5kg) acceleration time (determined largely by power/weight ratio) which are close to, or a little better than, the 7.1sec which *Motor* recorded for the 246.

At high speeds the position changes, since a good 246 will pull maximum revs (7,800rpm — just over the 7,600rpm maximum *power* revs) in fifth, giving a top speed of 148mph (238kph), whereas production versions of the 206 achieved around 143mph (230kph). The difference is a little bigger than can be accounted for by the cube law relating power required to aerodynamic drag, so perhaps the 180bhp power figure was indeed optimistic, or maybe the slightly greater overall length of the 246 gave it a marginally lower drag coefficient.

4 Production and Development

Production of the 206GT Dino did not actually begin until the middle of 1968, more than six months after it had been launched at the Turin Show of November 1967. Pininfarina played no part in the manufacturing process, their role being confined to design and to final development in conjunction with Ferrari. The tubular steel chassis, built by a small local engineering company, was taken to the Scaglietti works in Modena where it was fitted with the aluminium body panels. The completed bodyshell was then painted and transferred to Ferrari's Maranello factory for final assembly and finishing. At that stage in the project the engine/transmission unit was both made from Fiat parts — all the castings are clearly stamped 'Fiat' — and assembled by Fiat. All cars were built in left-hand drive form, and the chassis number of the first production is now believed to be 00104.

A few months after production had begun, the car (still only in left-hand drive form) became available in Britain, making its first appearance in the new car price list of *Motor*'s 9 November 1968 issue. So heavy has inflation been since those days that the price asked — £6,110 including taxes — now seems ridiculously low. But by the standards of the time the 206 was an expensive car, for although a 365GTB4 cost a good deal more at £8,563, as did a Rolls-Royce Silver Shadow at £7,790, a Jaguar XJ6 4.2 cost only £2,254 and a Ford Zephyr Zodiac V6 Executive just £1,678, while at the bottom of the scale the price of a Fiat 500 was £471 and of a Mini was £561. Interestingly, though, whereas the 206 was roughly three times the price of a Jaguar saloon, the current (summer 1989) Ferrari 328GTB is only about twice as expensive as a modern Jaguar XJ6 3.6.

Production built up to a rate of about three cars per week, so that in January 1969 Paul Frère was able to ride briefly in the 85th car made, though most of his test (see page 58) was based on his experiences with the first production car, owned by Sergio Pininfarina. But almost as soon as it appeared, the 206 began to look obsolete alongside the rival Porsche 911 which was steadily gaining engine capacity and performance. By the summer of that year, therefore, production ceased, to make way for the more powerful 246. Ferrari chassis numbers (see separate story — page 85) present many mysteries but studies conducted by *Ferrari Register* author Robert Abraham and American enthusiast Denny Schue currently confirm earlier estimates that approximately 150 206GTs were built altogether, and it is known with certainty that five of these left-hand drive cars were imported new into Britain.

INTRODUCTION OF THE 246 — SERIES I

The more powerful 246 model, though revealed at the Geneva Show of March 1969, did not begin to come off the production lines until soon after its proper launch at the Turin Show in the November of the same year. It retained the centrelock knock-off wheels of the 206, was built by much the same methods as before, and at a similar rate. It replaced the 206 in *Motor*'s price list of 9 December and, still in left-hand drive form at that stage, was at first available at the same price as the 206, which by then had risen to £6,242. Other cars had been subject to similar price increases, the 365GTB costing £9,167 compared to £9,272 for a Silver Shadow and £2,690 for a Jaguar XJ6 4.2.

With a few exceptions to be described in due course, no major changes were made to the 246 throughout its life. But the basic design was subjected to almost constant modification in detail, and not all the alterations were formally recorded. Some, however, are identified in workshop manuals and spare parts catalogues which separate the production run into three series: Type L or Series I, Type M or Series II, and Type E or Series III. The first of these three series finished with chassis number 01116, when some 357 cars had been built.

PRODUCTION RATE INCREASES – SERIES II

The second production series began with a fundamental change to manufacturing methods. Following the injection of Fiat capital after their take-over of Ferrari in August 1969, a large extension to the Maranello factory was built which became operational in September 1970. The extra space was used to make room for three production lines, the first of which was for the final assembly of the Fiat Dino, hitherto assembled at Fiat's Rivolta plant. On the second production line the V6 engine, previously put together by Fiat, was also assembled, though still from Fiat parts. And on the third line the Ferrari Dino was, as before, assembled, but at a significantly higher rate.

For this second production run – which started at chassis number 01118 – the modifications to the car included the substitution of bolt-on in place of knock-off

---

Ferrari chassis numbers

Ferrari single-seaters have always had separate chassis numbering systems, but after the first couple of years of production, a nominally consistent approach was adopted for the other cars made: those primarily intended for racing were allotted even numbers, two apart, whereas those destined for the road were assigned odd numbers, two apart.

But a new series of even five-figure chassis numbers, two apart and starting at 01000, was created for the Dino. This series was continued for the successor to the 246 Dino, the 308GT4, making it difficult to determine exactly when production of one finished and the other began.

Unfortunately there are many other anomalies because Ferrari appear to have been distinctly casual in their attitude towards chassis numbering. For example, numbers seem to have been assigned to chassis at the start of their production and take no account of the subsequent build time which could vary by anything up to several weeks, so that a car with a later number may have been completed and sold before a car with an earlier number. Robert Abraham, author of the *Ferrari Register,* in Britain, and Denny Schue in the States are two authorities on these arcane matters to which hundreds of hours of research have been devoted.

---

wheels and a change from Girling to Ate disc brakes. Soon after the new factory extension had been commissioned, the first right-hand drive model (chassis number 01134) became available – at the 1970 London Motor Show. With its steel body, cast iron cylinder block and plastic-trimmed interior (leather was an optional extra) it was seen as a car of lower specification than the 206, and in recognition of this its price was reduced to £5,486 a few weeks later. The handful of 206 owners, however, who had mostly paid nearly £1,000 more for their cars, were not enthusiastic supporters of this philosophy.

A Pininfarina-styled Dino 206GT of 1969 vintage.

At some stage, the front bumpers were exchanged for a new type which stopped short of the central air intake instead of curving into it. This is said to have happened at chassis number 01250 but some much later cars have the supposedly early bumpers. Chassis number 02130, assigned to a car believed to have been built in around July 1971, marked the end of Series II production. Whereas the 357 cars of Series I had been produced in just under a year, 507 Series II cars were built in a slightly shorter period, demonstrating the increased production rate. As a result, Ferrari's total annual output, including the bigger V12 cars, began to rise quite significantly, from 619 in 1969, to 928 in 1970 and 1,246 in 1971.

SERIES III

With the beginning of Series III production at chassis number 02132 came a further increase in production rate, bringing Ferrari's total output to 1,844 for 1972, though it dropped slightly to 1,772 for 1973. Some 3,019 cars altogether were produced in this final batch which came to an end in 1974 at chassis number 08518 when the 308GT4 was introduced (see Chapter 6).

The modifications incorporated in Series III cars included small changes to the ratios of the transfer and final drive gears and to the gearbox ratios, though the overall ratio for each gear remained much the same (see Specifications — page 34). The fuel supply system and crankcase breathing arrangement were also changed.

THE 246GTS

At the Geneva Motor Show of March 1972 an additional 246 model was introduced in the form of an open version with a Targa-type roof panel which could be detached and stowed behind the seats. It was called the 246GTS, the S standing for Spider, the traditional Continental name for open sporting cars, and which was originally often applied to horsedrawn vehicles of a similar character.

For this model a rollover hoop above the seats was created by strengthening the remaining strip of fixed roof at the back of the cockpit and giving it additional support each side through the removal of the two small windows in the external surfaces of the rear fairings — at some sacrifice in three-quarter rear visibility. These fairings were therefore fabricated from continuous sheet metal, unbroken save for three small slots each side which matched the existing slots in the bonnet. Although the steel body of the 246 makes a relatively small contribution to the overall stiffness, the removal of the roof did entail some loss of torsional rigidity, and so to compensate for this the chassis was strengthened, notably with additional bracing in the frame immediately ahead of the engine and extra stiffening for the chassis side members.

The GTS was produced solely in the Series III production run starting (so it is believed) at chassis number 03022 (03688 was the first right-hand drive GTS). The 246 Spider proved to be very popular, particularly in Britain and the United States, a total of 1,274 being built altogether (some authorities feel that 'Spider' should be spelt with a 'Y' but Ferrari themselves often spelt it with an 'I').

THE UK MARKET

In Britain the idea of creating a (relatively) inexpensive Ferrari to attract more people to the marque succeeded admirably. The average buyer was very similar to the average buyer of a 'big' Ferrari, but younger, at an earlier stage in his or her career and with a smaller income. A professional man or woman or the sole proprietor of a business were typical purchasers, says Mark Konig,

who was on the sales staff of the UK importers, Maranello Concessionaires Ltd, at the time and is now Sales Director of the company. So great was the enthusiasm displayed by such customers that the UK became one of the best markets for the Dino, taking around 504 GT models and 242 GTS models by the time production finished — that was nearly twenty per cent of the 3,883 cars believed to have been manufactured altogether.

But the success of the car did not depend upon the wide range of options available for it. Electric window lifters were available from the factory but all cars imported into Britain were fitted with these as non-optional extras which had to be paid for (they added £83.55 with tax to the price in 1971). Many variations were possible though, for the seats, door trims, central console and engine bulkhead which could be covered in leather as an optional extra, while even for the standard plastic trim there was a choice of black, blue, red or tan. And the external paintwork was available in an unusually wide selection of colours, which ranged from Rosso, the classic Ferrari red, to Nero, from Bianco Polo Park to Azzurro Dino. Numerous 'metallizzato' colours were also available, at extra cost though (see Appendix — page 187).

A small 'nosebar', was an extra created by the concessionaires for the UK market only. Transparent plastic headlamp fairings were also made available, again exclusively for the UK market, by Maranello Concessionaires, though these were only used experimentally by the factory and were found to make a negligible difference to the top speed — but to create, however, a noticeable deterioration in headlamp performance. Quite late in the overall production run, in around 1972, a 'Daytona' option package became available, involving seats that were similar in style to those of the bigger V12 model plus wider wheels and rather crudely styled flared wheelarches.

The nose-bar (above) and headlight fairings (below) are both British market options.

A rare photograph (below) of an AE-Brico electronic fuel injection system with which the Ferrari engineers experimented for the US market. The system was not adopted for the Dino, but saw brief production in such cars as the Aston-Martin DB6.

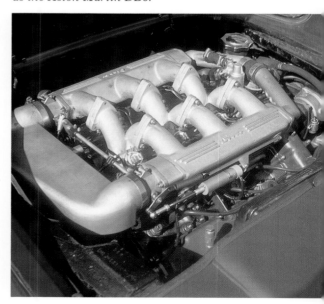

The 246GT Spider was launched at the Geneva Motor Show of 1972. This particular model dates from 1974.

THE US MARKET

The difficulties of meeting American exhaust emission and safety regulations delayed the introduction of the 246 to the US until 1972 when both the GT and the GTS models became available. The Ferrari engineers are known to have experimented with fuel injection to meet the American requirements for exhaust cleanliness, but settled for an arrangement involving a pump which injected air into the exhaust ports.

This was a common solution, both for European and American manufacturers in those days – when the approach to exhaust emission control was quite crude. Controls on oxides of nitrogen (generated by high combustion temperatures) had not then been introduced, so the emphasis was on the reduction of the levels of carbon monoxide (CO) and unburned hydrocarbons (HC). Since both these pollutants are the products of incomplete combustion, the technique generally adopted was to inject air into the exhaust ports so that the combustion that had started in the cylinders could be completed outside them but before the exhaust gases left the engine. Paradoxically, the engine was often deliberately fed with an over-rich mixture to 'seed' the external combustion reaction which either took place in the exhaust manifold or in a 'thermal reactor' – simply a chamber kept at a high temperature in which the gases swirled about and were given time to finish the process. At idle, when it is particularly difficult to achieve complete combustion, the process was carried a stage further, additional fuel *and air* being supplied. To curb the resultant tendency for the revs to rise and power to be generated when it was not wanted – very embarrassing in cars fitted with automatic transmission – the ignition was retarded.

The US market 246 Dino, therefore, was fitted with the necessary air injection pump driven through an electromagnetic clutch which disengaged at 3,500rpm (because emission control largely applies to idling and low-speed running). An idling ignition retard system controlled by engine oil temperature was fitted, with a microswitch override that brought it out of action when a preset throttle opening was exceeded.

While the net result of these arrangements was certainly a decrease in the HC and CO levels, the penalty, as for most cars of the period treated in the same way, was reduced power, increased fuel consumption and poor drivability. *Road and Track* quoted a maximum power of 175bhp instead of 195bhp, and in conjunction with an increase in weight due to safety as well as emissions requirements, this cut in output had a noticeable effect on performance. The 0–60mph (0–96.5kph) acceleration time obtained by *Road and Track* was 7.9sec compared to *Motor*'s 7.1sec, for instance, and the 0–100mph (161kph) time was 21.5sec instead of 17.6sec. Similarly, the fuel consumption had deteriorated from 16.1mpg to 15.3mpg (12.7 miles per US gallon) in driving conditions which almost certainly were less demanding than those of Europe. Performance and economy would have been further blunted on cars fitted with the optional air conditioning system made available for the US market. *Road and Track* also complained of poor drivability, saying 'the unit is decidedly unhappy at low speeds, bucking and misfiring to prove it'.

The Americans criticised the gearchange, too, and found the engine unreasonably loud. And in the States the Dino was again expensive, costing $14,500 in basic form (East Coast price; $13,885 West Coast) compared to $9,800 for a de Tomaso Pantera and $8,145 for a five-speed Porsche 911E.

Despite these disadvantages, most American journalists remained generally enthusiastic about the car. 'Traffic conditions, speed limits and roads are such that cars of even moderately high capabilities can seldom be used to their limits', wrote *Road and Track*'s reporter, 'Yet it is a thrill to drive a car like the Dino, one whose capabilities are far beyond what even an expert driver can use in most real-world motoring, and that is the Dino's reason for being.' *Motor Trend* wrote in similar vein, saying 'You begin to do things that you wouldn't dream of doing in a lesser machine. Every curve seems ironed out and the pace of life gets faster than you ever thought possible'.

THE DINO IN RACING

With its high performance and superb handling the Dino almost begs to be taken out on a circuit, yet, very surprisingly, it was hardly ever used for competition when in production. Today, though, a number of owners race their cars in the Maranello series of events (see Chapter 8) specially devised for classic Ferrari enthusiasts.

One notable break in that early neglect of the Dino's sporting potential occurred in 1972 when a 246GT was entered for the Le Mans 24-hour race by Luigi Chinetti's North American Racing Team, usually known by its initials, NART. The 246 was entered in the Group 4 class for production-based cars, and was fitted with the Daytona option package which included wider wheels and flared wheelarches – indeed, it has been suggested that the Daytona package was specifically created to make it possible for the car to be more competitive in Group 4. Additional slots in the front bonnet lid – to help air escape from the radiator – and a

It comes as a surprise to learn that the Dino 246 was hardly used competitively during its production life.

small air dam under the nose were among the modifications. In a race marred by the death of Jo Bonnier in a Lola, the car was driven by Laffeach and Doncieux and finished 17th — a creditable performance, especially since other Group 4 cars included 550bhp de Tomaso Panteras and 7-litre Chevrolet Corvettes as well as some Ferrari Daytonas.

FAMOUS OWNERS

The Dino's debut as a 'junior' Ferrari did not quite give it the status-object appeal sought by celebrities that was to be found in more powerful or bigger cars such as a 'full-sized' V12 Ferrari or a Rolls-Royce. So the list of early owners is not a roll-call of the rich and famous, though some of each certainly bought the car.

In the early seventies the Dino achieved fame of a sort by featuring in the TV series *The Persuaders* (1971–1972) starring Tony Curtis and Roger Moore. Then came the fuel crisis and, along with many other high-performance cars, the Dino plunged in secondhand value to ridiculously low levels.

Since then, an awareness of the Dino's

The 206SP was an accomplished racer in the late 1960s.

A personalised number-plate is nothing unusual when it is affixed to a Ferrari!

fundamental excellence — always evident to discerning observers — has gradually spread to increasing numbers of enthusiasts. In the long term, therefore, the Dino has won itself a solid reputation so that past and present owners include such celebrities as Peter Palumbo, Nick Mason, Prince Michael of Kent, Eric Clapton, Max Aitken and John Hugenholtz.

5 The Fiat Dino

When Giovanni Agnelli of Fiat decided to build power units for Ferrari he set his engineers a formidable task. The agreement announced in March 1965 gave them a mere two years to build 500 engines of a kind very different from their normal production units. For a big company like Fiat the number must have been an awkward one. The experimental department could perhaps build ten completely new power units in the time available, maybe even twenty-five if stretched, but 500 was a quantity big enough to require serious tooling and production design effort, yet small enough to be a nuisance to an organisation accustomed to building engines in hundreds of thousands per year. It is for similar reasons that many companies were later to set up special divisions for the small-volume production of sporting or high-performance variants; Ford's SVE (Special Vehicle Engineering) operation is just one example.

But building the Ferrari light alloy V6 engine was only part of the requirement: they also had to find a car to put it in, since the new Formula 2 regulations specified that the power units eligible for it must be based on a 'production engine installed in at least 500 cars'. At that time, however, few of Fiat's existing or planned cars looked a suitable recipient for such an advanced and sporting engine. The rear-engined 500 and 850 models were clearly quite inappropriate, while the mid-range cars such as the 1500 saloon were too stodgy to benefit from an aristocratic implant and the new 124, then being prepared for launch a year later, too downmarket. Only the 2300S coupe could have been considered a candidate.

The issue must have been confused by the existence at the planning stage of an open sports version of the 124, to be called the Fiat 124 Sport Spider and to be launched a few months after the saloon upon which it was based. It was to be endowed with a graceful body styled by Pininfarina, and to be given considerable glamour and excitement by its twin cam engine — a variant of an existing Fiat four-cylinder unit. To compensate for the reduction in torsional rigidity created by its open bodywork, this new model was to be provided with a special platform chassis, considerably stiffer than the 124 saloon's, with box-section side members of around twice the depth, a heavy box-section cross member at the rear and stiffened wheelarch structures.

Despite the marketing problems that might have been created, Fiat decided to design a second open sports car specially to fit the Ferrari V6 engine. The result was the Fiat Dino which first appeared, a week or two after the Fiat 124 Spider, at the Turin Show of November 1966. Like the 124 Spider it was an open sports car, and its body was also styled by Pininfarina. But the 124 Spider was clearly seen as an opportunity to cut design and tooling effort rather than as a potential sales conflict, for there is a marked similarity between its platform chassis and the Fiat Dino's. The two cars share not merely the same general front engine/rear-wheel drive layout, but also an identical wheelbase. Production problems were further eased by sub-contracting the manufacture as well as the styling of the Fiat Dino Spider body to Pininfarina.

Engineering problems aside, the association with Ferrari came at a good time for Fiat which had reached an important turning point in its development. To begin with, it had become one of the largest motor manufacturers in Europe, producing more than one million vehicles in 1966, the year the Fiat Dino and 124 Spider were introduced. But in addition it was preparing for fundamental changes in the pattern of demand. Its success after the Second World War largely depended upon its inexpensive but characterful transport-for-the-masses models such as the Fiat 500. But the public in Italy and elsewhere were beginning to demand something more than basic transport, and Fiat's middle-range 1300 and 1500 saloons were rather dull, heavily understeering cars with no sparkle to them. The 124, even though it retained the conventional layout of the day with a live rear axle, was considerably more up to date in character as well as styling, and represented a stage in a sweeping modernisation programme and rapid expansion of the model range. Between March 1966 and April 1967, Fiat introduced no fewer than seven new models differing substantially from one another in bodyshell or mechanical components, or both. They were the 1100R, the 124 saloon, the 124 Spider, the Dino Spider, the 124 coupe, the Dino coupe and the 125 saloon.

During these final years of the sixties, therefore, Fiat revitalised its image and acquired a much more sporting reputation with a range that included the 850 Spider and coupe, plus a number of Abarth-tuned variants of other models as well as the Dinos and 124 sport models already mentioned. The change in attitudes within the organisation was quite marked: service managers and mechanics were sent to Piero Taruffi's racing driver school to become familiar with a new generation of Fiat road cars that had sharper handling and better roadholding than their predecessors.

In all this the ability to produce a prestige sports car powered by a genuine Ferrari engine played a very useful part. Unquestionably Fiat gained considerable kudos of just the right sort from their association with Enzo and his products.

FIRST THOUGHTS

In its initial form as introduced at the 1966 Turin Show the Fiat Dino was a simple, even crude, car. By far the most sophisticated part of it was its front-mounted Ferrari V6 engine. This drove the rear wheels through a five-speed gearbox and a live rear axle mounted on leaf springs – an arrangement which was thought outdated and inappropriate, even at the time. Almost certainly, however, this simple form of rear suspension was chosen to save time. There is further evidence of haste and unfinished details in the reluctance of Fiat to allow close inspection of the car when it was first put on display at Turin. *Motor*'s Technical Editor at the time, Charles Bulmer, was forced to go on hands and knees to confirm that the car did indeed have a live rear axle. Not until some four months later, in February 1967, did Fiat release full technical details.

As already recorded (see Chapter 2) the Fiat Dino was at this stage fitted with the same 2-litre light alloy version of the 65deg V6 Ferrari engine as was to power the 206GT mid-engined Dino. With a bore and stroke of 86×57mm it had a capacity of 1,987cc and was identical to the Ferrari version save for carburetter settings and exhaust system details, yet it was said to produce only 160bhp at 7,000rpm compared to the 180bhp at 8,000rpm claimed for its rival. In its Fiat application it was, of course, longitudinally orientated as well as mounted at the front of the car, a conventional sump being bolted on in place of the transaxle developed for the mid-engined Ferrari Dino.

With its flywheel thus exposed in the ordinary way, a bell housing and gearbox was mounted on the back of the engine in the manner conventional for the period. The gearbox, a five-speed all-synchromesh unit,

A magnificently-polished, gleaming Fiat Dino Spider, as it appeared upon its launch at the Turin Show in November 1966.

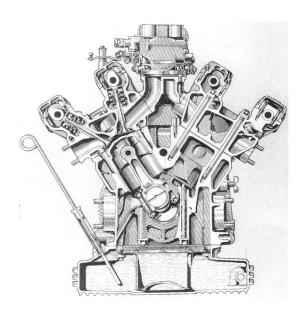 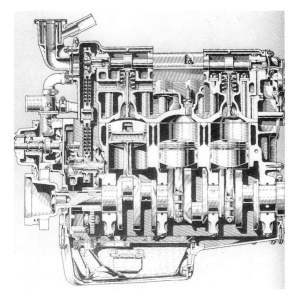

The 2-litre 65 deg V6 in Fiat Dino form.

was similar in design to the gearbox of the 124 Sport and incorporated parts from various Fiat sources including a 2300 casing. Essentially it was a four-speed unit with a fifth ratio housed in a small extension. From this unit the drive was taken via an open propeller shaft to a live rear axle incorporating a limited-slip differential.

At the front unequal-length double-wishbone suspension was fitted, with a wide-based single-piece upper wishbone upon which the coil spring and telescopic damper acted. The lower wishbone was divided into a transverse link and a leading brake reaction rod. A substantial anti-roll bar coupled the two hub carriers together. The steering was of the worm and peg sort, with a steering column shaft incorporating two universal joints to ensure collapsibility in an accident. There was a three-piece track rod and an idler lever incorporating a steering damper. Both suspension and steering were mounted on an insulated subframe.

As already noted, the adoption for a prestige high-performance car of a live rear axle — outdated even then — was greeted with some surprise, and even more so was the associated use of traditional leaf springs. The decision was made odder still by the more elaborate suspension system developed for the live axle of the 124 Spider which involved coil springs with a torque tube and radius arms providing fore-and-aft location, while a Panhard rod ensured lateral location.

But there were nevertheless some subtleties in the Dino's system which, to cut design effort, were probably borrowed from the arrangement already devised for the Fiat 125, to be launched in April 1967. The wide single-leaf springs which provided lateral location were mounted beneath the axle under spacer blocks to bring the rear roll centre down below hub height and additional (fore-and-aft) location was provided by a pair of short upper trailing radius arms. To control tramp movements, each end of the axle was straddled by a pair of dampers.

Ventilated disc brakes were fitted all round and were actuated via a servo through hydraulic circuits with a front/rear split and a load-sensitive rear pressure-relief valve to prevent premature lockup of the back wheels. These wheels, like those at the front, were of the centrelock type, made of light alloy, and had 6.5in (16.5cm) rims carrying 185-14 Michelin XAS tyres.

The Pininfarina body was differentiated from the 124 Spider's by being a good deal more curvaceous. It featured a low nose with four headlamps between higher wheelarches reminiscent of the first (Ferrari) Dino styling exercise, the Dino Berlinetta of 1965. The waistline crease in the flanks of the car was also reminiscent of the other Dino in its later and more developed form. Small occasional rear seats were fitted, the car was well equipped and nicely trimmed and weighed 22.5cwt (1145kg) unladen.

REACTIONS

The Fiat Dino was neither built by the factory in right-hand drive form nor imported into Britain on a regular basis. Contemporary English-language road impressions of the car are therefore rare, and the report we reproduce here – written by Charles Bulmer of *Motor* about the original model – is one of the few that do exist. He praises it for its straight-line performance, high-speed refinement and comfortable ride, but criticises its handling.

THE HOOD DOESN'T FLAP AT 130 . . .
Reproduced from *Motor* 18 March 1967

Driving the Fiat Dino

The Fiat Dino could become one of the really popular high performance sports cars of our time – whether it will depends on its cost; although 500 cars should have been made by the time these impressions appear, the price has yet to be decided. Production is urgent since this is the engine which must be homologated for the Ferrari Formula 2 car this year in which guise its four camshaft 1,987cc V6 engine (86×57mm.) will appear with an even shorter stroke to bring the capacity within the 1,600cc limit. Money isn't so urgent because Fiat have had a record-breaking year. 'Perhaps we'll deliver the cars first and send the bills later', they said.

Obviously, the light alloy engine is the expensive part. Except for a few modifications to ease production it is built exactly to the Ferrari blueprints, even retaining such features as connecting rods which are machined all over. Wherever possible, production components from other Fiats are used in the rest of the chassis; the gearbox, for example, has the 2300 casing and is machined on the same transfer line but has entirely special insides with three different kinds of synchromesh and a rear extension containing the geared-up fifth speed.

Bearing in mind that this is no lightweight competition car but a rather luxurious 22½cwt tourer with a feeling of extreme solidity and sturdiness, the performance figures are remarkable. Admittedly they were recorded solo, which gives a two hundredweight advantage over the standard Motor road test load, but even allowing for this the Dino steps straight on to a peak in the 2-litre class which was previously occupied only by the Porsche 911.

The figures speak for themselves – in terms of standing start acceleration and maximum speed there isn't much difference between the Dino and, say, the 7-litre Oldsmobile Toronado or Buick Riviera but the manner is quite different. It would be difficult to think of any sports car engine more enjoyable to possess – its tickover is a little bit lumpy and erratic and it doesn't like full throttle below 2,000rpm but it gets properly into its stride at 3,000rpm and it runs to the beginning of

A view of the Fiat Dino Spider, this model dating from 1967.

the red sector at 8,000 with silky six-cylinder smoothness. This represents a wider range of torque than you would expect from any engine giving a specific output of 80bhp per litre: it isn't in any way temperamental when you drive it slowly through rush-hour Turin and Fiat are expecting to improve its flexibility further in the next few weeks.

Nor is it noisy if you define noise as 'unwanted sound'. There is some clatter at tick-over, more audible outside than in, but as the revs go up this quickly changes to a typical Ferrari sound — the whirr of smooth high efficiency machinery surmounted by a slight whine from the long duplex timing chain (which drives all four camshafts) and backed by a discreet rasp from the exhaust. It all adds

up to a level which enables you to judge your gear-changes perfectly without ever becoming obtrusive at high speed on the autostrada.

It is, in fact, one of the most relaxing autostrada cars we've met, partly because the engine feels entirely unstrained at a steady 110–115mph and partly because of the suspension which, although we haven't yet mentioned it, is one of the more remarkable features of the car. Aided perhaps by the large 185-14 Michelin XAS tyres on 6½in rims, it possesses out-standingly good directional stability at any speed and a quality of ride which lifts it right out of the normal sports car class. It certainly isn't soft or wallowy but it accepts anything that the Italian roads can give it — which is

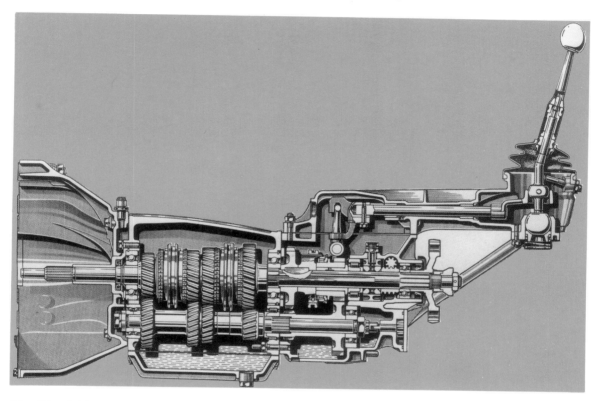

Fiat Dino MkI gear box.

plenty — and converts it into a flat, controlled pitch-free movement which is extremely pleasant. What is more, it does all this with a singular lack of road noise and harshness and the roadholding, in the true sense of keeping the wheels on the ground, is absolutely first class even when driving hard on the bumpy mountain roads between Alba and Savona in northern Italy.

Fiat engineers give a lot of credit to the XAS tyres. They say that they tried practically all the radial ply tyres available but they could find nothing else which combined equally good low speed characteristics with the ability to run safely at sustained speeds over 130mph on standard tyre pressures — about 25lb/sq.in.

In other words, if you didn't know that the Dino had a live axle at the rear you would

think it had very good independent suspension all round. Unfortunately, like most cars, it is not perfect: handling which is good for normal brisk driving becomes less so when you press it harder on corners. It seems to have a basic understeer — strong enough to make the front Michelins scream at the beginning of a bend — on which is super-imposed a roll oversteer and considerable throttle sensitivity; a little power tightens the radius noticeably, more power in second or third gears tends to break the back wheels away rather sharply and it is not easy to use this effect delicately on slow to medium corners because the accelerator has a sticky and rather sudden initial opening action.

The rear axle is located by single leaf springs and upper radius arms which together form, in effect, Watt linkages at

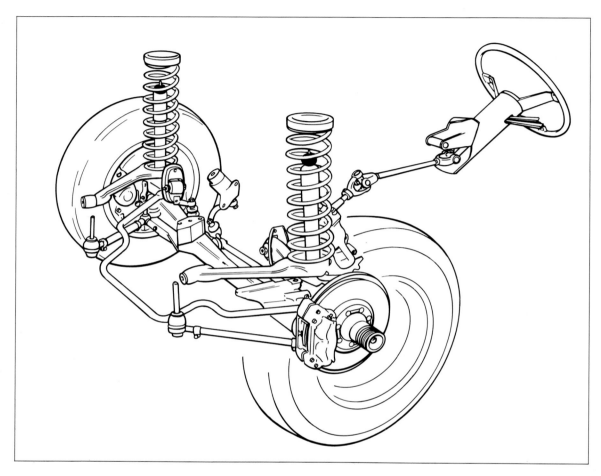

Fiat Dino front suspension. Conventional wishbone and anti-roll bar arrangement with coil spring/damper units on top of the upper wishbone.

each side: the static geometry of the rear suspension is such that we believe that the rear axle tries to twist in roll — in other words it becomes an extremely powerful anti-roll bar — and this may well be the reason for these characteristics. It still gets round corners quite quickly but not as quickly as some sportscars we know, nor does it inspire as much confidence in the driver; it might become rather tricky on wet roads although the weather didn't allow us to confirm or deny this suspicion.

Steering is on the heavy side for parking although very light and accurate as soon as you get moving. The brakes are equally light — perhaps a little too much so because you only have to touch them gently to stop quite rapidly from any speed: this is the first European production car we can bring to mind with ventilated discs and they are made under American Kelsey-Hayes patents although the rest of the system is largely Girling.

A good sports car engine deserves a five-speed gearbox and this Fiat has one of the best; the first four gears are arranged in the

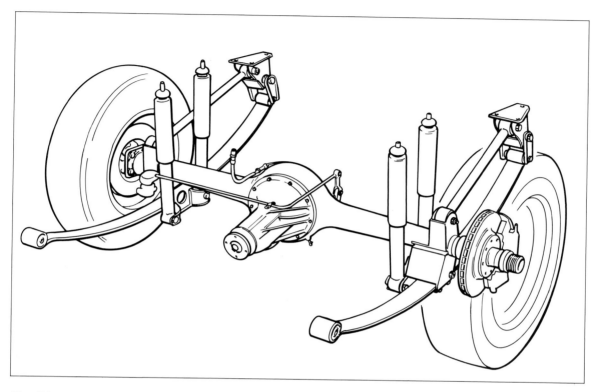

Fiat Dino MkI rear suspension. Live rear axle with additional location by upper radius arms.

conventional four-speed pattern with fifth 'round the corner' — forward and to the right. Each gear gives roughly another 25mph at 8,000rpm and fifth is not an overdrive cruising ratio — it is correctly geared for maximum speed; five-speed boxes can be spoiled by poor arrangement of the gate and selectors but this one is beautifully engineered for smooth, easy and extremely rapid changes with a minimum of familiarisation.

There's no need to say a lot about the body — it's designed and built to Pininfarina standards with every comfort and convenience you expect in an expensive touring car and one or two you don't expect like four quartz-iodine headlamps. The occasional rear seats are useful mainly for luggage or small children but the adjustable front seats are very comfortable; the driving position is typically Italian in that the steering wheel is almost too far away even for straight arms.

It took a long time to get the hood design right but it was worth the effort. It doesn't flap at 130mph, it doesn't make enough wind roar to stop you cruising at 115mph and you can put it up or down in a few seconds. Perhaps the sealing is a bit too good because the air flow through the heater increases enormously when you open a quarter light. But in the summer you can unzip the entire rear window panel of the hood which would probably be an ideal compromise for long distances. In fact, one way and another it would probably be difficult to find a more pleasant and less tiring way of crossing Europe in a hurry.

Charles Bulmer

PERFORMANCE

CONDITIONS
Dry, cool, negligible wind.
Fuel: 98–100 Octane (RM)
Driver only – no test kit.

MAXIMUM SPEEDS		m.p.h.
Mean of opposite runs (kilometre)		127.1
Best one-way kilometre		129.2
4th gear		113
3rd gear	at 8,000 r.p.m.	85
2nd gear		60
1st gear		35

ACCELERATION TIMES	
m.p.h.	sec.
0–50	6.8
0–100	22.5
0–110	27.8
Standing ¼-mile	16.2
Standing kilometre	29.4

SPEEDOMETER
4% fast at 50 m.p.h., 100 m.p.h. and maximum speed.

It's entirely possible that the Fiat engineers listened to Charles Bulmer's criticisms of the Dino Spider's handling and made some last-minute changes to the rear suspension. At any rate, when Paul Frère reported on the car a few weeks later, his reactions to its handling were a good deal more favourable:

CONTINENTAL DIARY

Reproduced from *Motor*
1 April 1967

For cost and service reasons respectively, the Fiat engineers would have liked to incorporate the cog belt camshaft drive and their novel valve adjustment (of the Fiat 124S – Ed) in the Dino engine, but Ferrari asked them not to, as he wanted to use the engine as a Formula 2 unit with as little modification as possible and, if he could help it, he did not like to race any device he had not tried under racing conditions before. In fact, the only concession he made to Fiat in the basic design of the engine was the use of a stronger crankshaft which would pass Turin's requirements of 500 hours under pre-determined conditions on the test bench. The development work to make the engine practical for everyday use was left to Fiat, and they did a very good job of making it a really tractable unit – I would say even more so than the present 2300S – without sacrificing too much of the ultimate power.

Many people who had a look under the Dino at the Turin Show were surprised to find a rigid axle and semi-elliptic springs in a brand new sports car said to be capable of around 130mph. The main reason for the use of such a suspension seems to have been pressure of time: in order to enable Ferrari to use the engine for his F.2 car, 500 Dinos had to be produced by the beginning of the current year, barely 18 months after the agreement had been concluded. Having no previous experience of i.r.s. for high performance cars, they felt they could probably solve the problem better in the time available by using a normal rear axle and drawing upon the resources made available by the latest developments of the tyre industry. The outcome – single leaf semi-elliptic springs with twin shock-absorbers each and reversed torque reaction arms forming a Watt linkage with the front part of the spring – is a result of a lot of headache (a Panhard rod had also been added, then discarded), but gives extremely satisfactory results in conjunction with 6½in. wide rims.

New Michelin XAS asymmetric or Pirelli Cinturato tyres are fitted, the Michelin being preferred by the works because they can be used at very low pressures – 24lb front and 26lb rear – even at sustained high speed, which is very important in the context of the suspension used. In fact, the whole set-up works extremely well. Comfort is as good as in any car of this kind and handling is extremely safe and predictable. Before going out on the Monza track, I felt suspicious about lapping as fast as the car would go on

*The Fiat Dino Spider clearly had very little in common with its
cousin at Ferrari.*

the low tyre pressures I was told to try before I raised them, but actually I put in about 20 laps, admittedly on a greasy surface, without ever getting the impression that harder tyres would improve the handling which was very safe and predictable. The Dino is set up to understeer slightly and there is practically no change of attitude if the throttle is closed suddenly in a curve though, on a greasy surface, there is enough power to drive the car as much with the throttle as with the steering, control under these conditions being particularly good thanks to the limited slip differential.

On winding mountains roads also — and still with the same tyre pressures — the car proved to be very agile and a lot of power can be applied while the vehicle is still rounding a sharp corner without inducing wheel spin. One probable reason for this we found when, trying a few standing starts, it was discovered that the rear suspension geometry was such that the torque reaction would actually raise the tail of the car and thus push the wheels hard on the ground the moment full torque was applied.

Incidentally, while on the 124 Spider the fifth gear is a real 'overdrive' in the sense that it is a cruising gear on which the engine will never reach its peak rpm, maximum speed being obtained in fourth, the indirect fifth of the Dino is geared for maximum speed peak revs (7,900) being reached at the highest speed the car will reach on the level.

BERTONE COUPE

Right from the start of the Fiat Dino project, Pininfarina created a coupe version of the car — effectively a Spider with an integrated hardtop. But it was Pininfarina's rivals, Bertone, who were awarded the contract to style and build closed bodies for the Fiat Dino. Fully as graceful as the Spider, but in a different way, the Bertone coupe appeared in the spring of 1967, a few months after the

Spider had been launched. It was a considerably more roomy car with proper rear seats thanks to a wheelbase longer by 4in (10cm). In all other respects, however, it was mechanically identical to the Spider.

THE 2400 FIAT DINOS

At the Turin Show of November 1969 the Fiat Dino Spider and Coupe appeared with a number of important improvements. To begin with, both cars got the new iron-block version of the Ferrari V6 engine with its larger capacity of 2,418cc. For the Fiat Dino this meant an increase in power from 160bhp at 7,600rpm for the old 2-litre unit to 180bhp at 6,600rpm for the new 2.4 engine, while maximum torque was up from 126lb ft at 6,000rpm to 159lb ft at 4,600rpm. (The figures were a little higher for the Ferrari version of the engine — see page 33.)

These increases in power and torque exceeded the capacity of the original gearbox so a new ZF five-speed gearbox was fitted instead. As before, the final drive unit incorporated a limited-slip differential, but one of a different type and design. It incorporated a centrifugal control system which unlocked the differential at high road speeds to allow some spinning of the inside rear wheel in bends; this tends to slow the car and prevent sudden breakaway, creating a fail-safe effect at the limit of adhesion. At lower speeds there was no inhibition of the differential's locking action, so that improved traction in snow and ice could be retained.

But perhaps the most important change was to replace the live axle with independent rear suspension. No longer under pressure to design and develop the car in haste as they had been originally, the Fiat engineers had been given time for second thoughts.

Their conclusion was to provide the Fiat Dino with an independent rear suspension similar to that devised for the Fiat 130 saloon

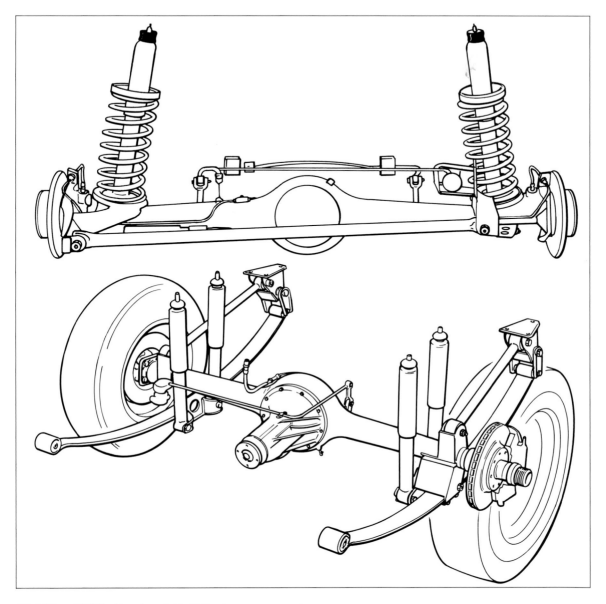

Fiat Dino MkI (bottom) *and 124S* (top) *rear suspensions compared.*

launched earlier in the year. This is often described as being of the semi-trailing arm kind, but in fact it is a form of MacPherson strut suspension in which the telescopic damper acts as a locating element, its bottom end being fixed rigidly to the top of the hub carrier. Transverse location of the bottom of the hub carrier is provided by a fixed-length drive shaft and a parallel radius arm behind

it to control bump-steer, while fore-and-aft location is provided by a long angled link of pressed steel which also forms the spring pan.

Other changes included wider, 70-profile tyres, bigger brakes and a small electric pump to maintain servo vacuum during prolonged braking — owners of the original cars had complained about running out of servo assistance when descending mountain passes. There were improvements to trim and equipment, too. The Bertone coupe, for instance, acquired improved ventilation and electric window lifters as a standard fitting rather than an option. It was upon this model that Paul Frère pronounced very favourably for *Motor* in his *Continental Diary*:

DRIVING THE NEW FIATS AT TURIN
by Paul Frère

Reproduced from *Motor*
8 November 1969

At his very interesting press conference, Gianni Agnelli, Fiat's President, stressed the fact that the development of his firm's sporting range of cars was part of the effort made to glamourize Fiat's image and to attract youth towards the cars made in Turin, even if they could not afford the more prestigious ones.

With Alfa-Romeo and Lancia (now part of the Fiat empire) also producing renowned sports models, this aim can only be achieved if the sporting range of cars is kept right up to date and on the occasion of the Turin Show just this has been done with both the 124 Sport and the Dino ranges. Though the strikes which have already cost Fiat 170,000 cars this year prevented the usual large number of demonstration cars being made available to the press, facilities were provided on the Torino-Ivrea Autostrada for timing the cars in both directions over flying and standing quarter mile and kilometre and I was also given a chance to take both a 124 Coupé and and Dino Coupé out on the road.

1,600cc 124 Sport

By dropping the 1,608cc engine of the 125S, in this case with a second twin choke carburetter,

into the existing 124 Sport, using a lower-geared final drive and stepping up the overdrive fifth, Fiat have now produced the car I used to wish for when I owned a 124 Spider. Thanks to the much better low-speed torque, one is much less tempted to rev the engine up to very high speeds (the red line is as high as 7,300rpm), which automatically makes the car much quieter, though quietness certainly has been improved in itself too; 20% higher torque and 5% lower gearing add up to much better acceleration on all four lower gears, while fifth still affords good acceleration together with a usefully high gearing, the engine turning over at 6,200rpm when I timed the Coupé at 112mph (one way, but with no wind at all) over the kilometre — exactly the maker's figure. With a standing start, I achieved 31.4sec over the kilometre at the first try, an improvement of over two seconds on my own test figure for the previous version of the car, and the overall impression gained both on the motorway and on the road is that of a much more effortless car.

The seats, now with the central section upholstered in cloth, are improved too and give excellent lateral support, as I found in the second part of the test, when I took the car over my favourite test course out of Turin, a quiet beautiful winding road in the mountains with all sorts of curves, many of them affording very good visibility. The 124 Sport has earned a reputation for quite exceptionally good handling and high cornering power, but in this respect I thought the car tested did not quite live up to its reputation for it could have done with less understeer. The first series of 124 Sport which had a torque reaction tube were fitted with a small rear anti-roll bar and were nearly neutral steering cars. When the location of the rear axle was altered, which improved ride and reduced the transmission of road noise and vibrations, the anti-roll bar disappeared and the car understeered more. This tendency seems to have been increased

The Fiat Dino Coupé.

by the slightly heavier 1,600cc engine (which in turn, has called for slightly stiffer springs) in spite of the fact that the front anti-roll bar has been reduced by one millimetre in diameter. I personally would like to see the small rear anti-roll bar back in its place though it might then need a limited slip differential with the extra power now available. You have to stop adding cost somewhere . . . ! And cost has been added in the braking department too, which is now of the twin circuit system with a larger sized servo reducing the force to be applied on the pedal. It gives excellent response while maintaining very good feel and brutal downhill driving did not produce any fade.

Dino 2400 Coupé

The Dino with its V6, four-cam, Ferrari-designed engine has undergone much more radical changes than the 124 Sport. Only the body structure and the front suspension and steering have remained unchanged. The engine capacity has gone up from 2 to 2.4 litres with a cast iron cylinder block (instead of aluminium) adding 20Kg to the weight: the clutch is larger; a ZF 5-speed gearbox replaces the similar Fiat box which could not take the 25% higher torque of the bigger engine; the rear axle has been completely redesigned from rigid to independent; the brakes have been vastly improved and there are fatter, 70-profile tyres.

The character of the car has not changed however. The Ferrari rumble is still there and from the word go, the car invites keen driving. The engine certainly still thrives on revs, though there is little point in pushing it up to its very respectable 8,000rpm limit, but you don't feel the power coming in at 5,000 so much as you did with the old 2-litre, for there is now plenty of power available well below this, in spite of unchanged camshafts. In fact, if you feel like it, you can potter along in town traffic in direct fourth and get immediate response to the accelerator, though there is still a distinct flat spot around 2,000rpm — a range you wouldn't normally use on a car of this sort anyway. The additional 20hp has increased the maximum speed by about 5mph to 128–129mph reached at about 7,500rpm in fifth, and the gain in acceleration is quite considerable. Two-way timing over the standing quarter mile and the standing kilometre gave average times of 15.9 and 28.85 seconds, compared with my own test figures of 16.5 and 30.1 seconds respectively for the 2-litre version. This should produce a 0–100mph time around 20 seconds, and it must be borne in mind that the big gap and rather slow change from first to second on the new gearbox, which is certainly not as good as the old one, does not help fast standing start times.

As with the 124 Sport, the bigger and more flexible engine has resulted in a generally more effortless car, though the Dino can't by any means be called quiet: the Ferrari music is part of its character, while a lot of wind noise around a windscreen pillar was probably accidental, as it was noticed on one side only. But the best surprise certainly came when I took the car out on my mountain test course. When I knew that the Dino was to get independent rear suspension, my greatest fear was that the excellent handling of the original car might be spoiled, for I felt it would be difficult to improve on the original version. Well, I must admit the car is better with its new rear end for not only does it handle even better (part of which may also be due to the new tyres — Pirellis on the model I tried), but it is decidedly more comfortable with less unsprung weight to shake the body. While at speed on the Autostrada it goes as straight as an arrow, this rather heavy (3,000lbs) car would put a Mini to shame on winding roads, so beautifully balanced is it. Thanks to much less understeer, it actually felt lighter than the 900lbs lighter 124 Coupé while the throttle could be used to best advantage to help the back round, at cornering speeds not much short of

of what you would expect with racing tyres. An interesting device that is used to keep ham-footed drivers out of trouble is a limited slip differential which frees itself progressively thanks to a centrifugal device at higher speeds. This gives the benefit of the limited slip differential on snow and greasy going, but maintains the 'safety valve' effect of an inside spinning wheel if too much throttle is given in a bend.

The brakes too have been much improved, specially by the provision of an electric vacuum pump that prevents the servo running out of vacuum — a rather frightening experience I had several times with the old Dino, when the brake pedal felt like a piece of wood and nothing happened. Fade was also completely absent, in spite of the very hard time the brakes were given, evidenced only by the smoke they produced when we stopped.

Only detail changes have been made to the beautiful Bertone body. They include larger air outlets, better face-level ventilation and electric window lifters as standard.

PRODUCTION HISTORY

Although Fiat contracted out the manufacture of the Dino Spider to Pininfarina — and a little later that of the Coupe to Bertone — they were at first still left with the problems of manufacturing the engine and of final assembly of the complete cars which was done at the Rivolta factory. Some 1,163 Spiders and 3,760 Coupes were produced in this way with the original 2-litre engine.

From September 1970 onwards, however, manufacture of the new 2.4-litre engine and final assembly of the Fiat Dinos was transferred to the new extension of Ferrari's Maranello factory, where the mid-engined Dino was also put together. Although a much-improved car with more performance and independent rear suspension, the Fiat Dino didn't last long, going out of production in 1972 when a further 420 Spiders and 2,398 Coupes had been built.

6 Successors: 308GT4 and 308GTB

With the benefit of hindsight, it is often difficult to understand why certain classic models were ever taken out of production by their manufacturers. Many enthusiasts believe, for example, that, properly developed, not just the 246 Dino but a number of other cars such as the Jaguar E-type, the Lotus Elan and the Alfa Romeo Alfasud would be just as viable today as when they were first introduced. The continued existence of the Porsche 911 after more than twenty years of life tends to support the point.

But to the engineers and marketing men involved, things usually seemed very different at the time. Thus for Enzo Ferrari and his designers in the early seventies the fate of the Dino was threatened by a number of powerful pressures. It was that same Porsche 911 which represented one of the most important of them: the horsepower race. By the autumn of 1971 Porsche had enlarged their flat six engine from 2.2 litres to 2.4 litres (actually 2,341cc) raising the output of the most powerful variant in the range, the 911S, from 180bhp at 6,500rpm to 190bhp at the same speed, while maximum torque was up from 146lb ft at 5,200rpm to 181lb ft at 4,000rpm – a very substantial increase, greatly improving tractability.

With these improvements in power and torque the 911S began to gain a small but noticeable edge in acceleration over the heavier Dino, the Porsche's 0–60mph (0–96.5kph) acceleration time when tested by *Motor* being 6.2sec against the Dino's 7.1sec. Even though the German car still lagged slightly in top speed with a maximum of 145.3mph (234kph), its overall improvement in performance constituted a warning shot that could not be ignored.

The Ferrari V6 engine might perhaps have been increased in power to compete – one version of its immediate predecessor with four-valve combustion chambers had developed 300bhp for Tasman single-seater racing. Unfortunately the problem was not just to increase power but simultaneously to meet the American exhaust emission regulations, since sales in that country were of great importance. Meeting those regulations meant running on unleaded fuel which would not poison the catalytic converters that were becoming necessary. And the use of unleaded fuel of lower octane in turn enforced reduced compression ratios. Only by increasing engine capacity was it possible to compensate for the resultant loss of power. And since the regulations were becoming stiffer year by year, the engine needed for the future must be endowed with an ample reserve of capacity as well as the potential for considerably more power.

There were other reasons for believing that any replacement for the Dino would need a substantially bigger power unit. Even after its enlargement from 2 to 2.4 litres, the Dino's engine was a very high-revving unit which required extensive use of the gearbox to give of its best. But customers everywhere were demanding effortless acceleration without constant gearchanging, and high-speed cruising that was fuss-free and relaxed. Unreasonably, perhaps, they wanted their

The flamboyant curvaceousness of the late sixties was abandoned in favour of simpler, cleaner Bertone-styled lines which were not liked to begin with, but which earned respect over the years.

'junior' Ferrari to have more the sort of performance provided by the 'senior' Ferraris with their V12 engines of 4 litres or more.

A significantly bigger engine, though, was not the only requirement of a successor to the 246, because prestigious two-seaters have always been criticised for lack of space. Add a second pair of seats, no matter how vestigial, it is argued, and the appeal of the car is radically improved. At a stroke such a design change makes it possible to carry young children, satisfies the chairman who insists that all company cars must have four seats and meets — or at least softens — the objections of the wife seeking some modicum of practicality in the family vehicle. In theory the young business or professional man or woman owning such a car can then use it to take a couple of clients to lunch. In practice the 'occasional' rear seats which result from such thinking are usually only for show and quite uninhabitable by any human being bigger than a three-year old. Nevertheless the concept still has its adherents.

Two factors made the arguments behind it especially applicable to the Dino. Firstly, there's barely enough room behind the seats of a 246 Dino for a slim document case and a lightweight summer raincoat. Secondly, in this aspect of design the Dino's closest rival, the Porsche 911, scored yet again, since it had always been provided with the occasional rear seats that the salesmen demanded.

THE NEW DINO

Despite the commonplace nature of these arguments for more power and space, the 308GT4 which succeeded the Dino was greeted with some surprise and a little disappointment when it was announced in October 1973. Though still a mid-engined car and one with a transversely-orientated power unit and very similar transmission layout, but still badged as a Dino with (initially) no Ferrari insignia upon it, the

---

The prancing horse emblem

As explained in earlier chapters, there were initial fears — which quickly proved to be unjustified — that the original 206 and 246 models might not enhance the reputation of Ferrari. In consequence the Dino range of cars was denied, until part-way through the production run of the 308GT4, one of the most potent emblems ever to appear in the motoring world. Rolls-Royce's Flying Lady perhaps excepted, there can surely be no symbol more evocative or more quickly recognised than Ferrari's black prancing horse on a yellow shield. Everywhere in the world it is accepted as representing race-bred high performance and thoroughbred design.

The history of this *cavallino rampante* badge is quite complicated. Originally it was derived from part of the coat of arms of the *Piemonte Reale Cavalleria,* a crack cavalry regiment of northern Italy. As was common in all European armies in the early years of the century, this regiment became involved in aviation, allowing a certain young officer, Francesco Baracca, to become a flying instructor and test pilot. Early in World War I he qualified as an 'ace' with five kills and celebrated the occasion by adopting his regiment's prancing horse as a personal emblem painted on the side of his aircraft.

Francesco Baracca went on to notch up a total of thirty-four kills, but in June 1918 set off on a mission from which he never returned. After the war, however, his father, Enrico, became a customer of Enzo Ferrari when Enzo held an Alfa Romeo dealership. Ferrari came to know the prancing horse symbol, liked it, and approached Enrico Baracca for permission to use it. The permission granted, it appeared in slightly modified form for the first time in 1932 on the racing Alfa Romeos managed by the Scuderia Ferrari. Further minor changes followed, but from 1950 onwards the prancing horse badge, essentially in its present form, adorned all road-going (and most racing) Ferraris except, as already explained, the 206 and 246 Dinos and the early 308GT4s.

*The 308GT4 (above) was clearly descended from the 246 Dino
(below) but was, in most respects, a completely different car.*

new car differed from the 246 in three fundamental respects. To begin with it was powered by a completely new 3-litre light alloy four-camshaft 90deg V8 engine – the first eight-cylinder engine to be used for a road-going Ferrari. Next it had a 2 + 2 body with a pair of small occasional rear seats. These are the two design features summarised in the model designation: '308' meaning a three-litre eight-cylinder engine; 'GT' meaning, as usual, Gran Turismo; and '4' indicating four seats.

The third major difference lay in the character of that nominally four-seat body which was dramatically different in form and styled by Bertone rather than Pininfarina. In place of the multiplicity of flamboyant curves which distinguished the 246 there was a shape of severe and unadorned simplicity.

The increased accommodation was perhaps partly responsible for the lukewarm reception. Journalists were quick to criticise the almost complete lack of legroom for the new rear seats – 'it requires a good deal of optimism (and bad faith) to call the Dino a 2 + 2' wrote Paul Frère. Here Ferrari had created a problem for themselves, for while the new car kept the Dino name alive, it was not in fact a direct replacement for the 246. That was to be the two-seater 308GTB (see page 135) launched in October 1975. (The 'B' stands, rather illogically, for Berlinetta, meaning little saloon.) But although the 308GTB was styled, once more, by Pininfarina and inherited some of the body features of the 246, it was sold from the outset as a Ferrari, for by that time the Dino name had been dropped.

The same lack of enthusiasm extended to the style of the new body. Some thought that it had been a mistake to commission Bertone to style a Ferrari and wondered why they had been chosen instead of Pininfarina. The answer was that the arrival of Bertone coupe bodies for the Fiat Dino at Maranello had generated a respect for the rival stylist and coachbuilder which won them the contract.

Looking back, it's clear that Bertone were left with little alternative; any further development of the rounded form that had so distinguished the 246 was doomed to vulgarity and failure. A cleaner, simpler, shape – demanded in any case by the trends of the time – was the only possibility. Bertone nevertheless retained the rear air intakes to the engine compartment, but by moving them upwards to the bases of the rear pillars they became small gill-like apertures which contributed to the wholly different appearance of the car. The rearward-extending buttresses – more or less essential if a mid-engined car is to have a balanced appearance – were also retained, but the reverse-curvature rear screen was not. Instead, the rear quarterlights extended rearwards far enough to provide good three-quarter rear visibility and the rear screen is flat.

The body of shallow curves and flat planes into which these features were integrated was initially received with vague dissatisfaction. Only recently have enthusiasts begun to come to terms with the design and to appreciate the Bertone body for its excellent proportions and understated elegance.

INNOVATION WITH CONTINUITY

If there were reservations about the 2 + 2 accommodation and the body which provided it, the new power unit was greeted with nothing but respectful interest. Some observers perhaps harboured the vague feeling that the use of eight rather than six or twelve cylinders was a little out of character for Ferrari. It was not an opinion with much substance, however, since Ferrari had long before successfully designed and developed V8 engines for racing, notably the unit powering the 158 Formula 1 car with which John Surtees won both the Drivers' and Constructors' Grand Prix Championships in 1964.

Undoubtedly the experience thus gained proved useful when the 308 engine was engineered, though in its basic architecture it was a completely new design with a 90deg bank angle and a crankshaft running in five main bearings. Nevertheless it also shared features taken from other Ferrari power units. In its size and cylinder dimensions, for instance, it was effectively two-thirds of the 4.4-litre 365 V12 engine, with the same 81×71mm bore and stroke giving a capacity of 2,926cc. And following Ferrari's standard practice − from which the 246 engine had been a Fiat-imposed deviation − the new power unit had a very stiff light alloy block incorporating cast iron cylinder liners.

Like many other Ferrari engines, too, including its V6 predecessor, the 308 unit had combustion chambers of the hemispherical/pentroof type with overhead valves actuated by four camshafts through bucket tappets containing disc-shaped adjustment shims. As for the 246 engine, moreover, the combustion chambers were of the two-valve rather than four-valve type, the valves were set at a similar relatively narrow included angle (46deg) and single sparking plugs were used. These were fired by a conventional coil ignition system involving twin distributors driven off the inlet camshafts. Following a practice established for later versions of the 246, though, each distributor had two pairs of contact breaker points, one set 6deg retarded with respect to the other and used for low-speed running, a micro-switch actuated by opening the throttle controlling the changeover.

But a significant innovation for Ferrari − often conservative in design matters − was the use of toothed glass fibre drive belts in place of chains for the four camshafts, immediately following their adoption for the Berlinetta Boxer flat twelve engine. The decision to use them was probably influenced by research into their construction and operation which had been conducted by Aurelio Lampredi, once Ferrari's chief engine designer, but then working for Fiat. These belts were chosen partly because they were felt to be quieter running than chains, and partly because they do not need lubrication and timing cases and so simplify engine design. Because toothed belts are wider than equivalent timing chains, their adoption increases engine length slightly, but this is of little importance in the 308, since its power unit lies sideways in the chassis. Two separate belts were used, each with its own tensioner.

A pump on the crankshaft nose supplied oil for a wet sump lubrication system incorporating a separate oil cooler mounted in the engine compartment. Outboard of the camshaft drive belts, which were enclosed behind protective covers, a system of ordinary belts drove the water pump, the alternator and the air conditioning pump, if fitted. Four twin choke Weber 40DCNF carburetters were fitted, and with a compression ratio of 8.8:1 the new engine developed 255bhp at 7,600rpm with a maximum torque value of 210lb ft at 5,000rpm.

Set transversely in the car, this lusty new engine was coupled to a transmission system very similar to that of the 246. As before, the front part of the base casting of the transaxle forms the sump of the engine to which it is bolted, while the rear part is partitioned off to create an independent sump for the gearbox which has its own oil pump. From a conventional flywheel-mounted clutch the drive is passed downwards through three transfer gears to a quill shaft which forms an extension of the primary shaft of the five-speed all-synchromesh gearbox. Through a pair of final drive gears, the output shaft of this gearbox drives a limited-slip differential coupled to the two drive shafts. These are fitted with Rzeppa-type constant-velocity joints designed to accept plunge and so resolve the conflict of arcs between drive shaft and suspension linkage movement that would otherwise exist.

Bertone abandoned the reverse-
curvature rear screen of the 246 for a
flat rear screen on the 308GT4
(above), but maintained three-quarter
rear visibility by extending the two
back side windows rearwards (below).

Numerous colour and trim options
were available as extras (below).

Removal of the rear seats creates an optional luggage space
which is here concealed with a cloth.

In its suspension and running gear the 308GT4 was also a close relative of the 246. Unequal-length double-wishbone independent suspension very similar in geometry and construction was fitted all round, with the coil springs and concentric telescopic dampers bearing on the lower wishbones at the front, and, to clear the drive shafts, on the upper part of the hub-carrier at the rear. As before, too, the steering was by rack and pinion. The massive ventilated disc brakes were again very similar in size to those of the 246 (10.5in (26.6cm) in diameter at front; 10.75in (27.3cm) diameter at rear) and were actuated through a vacuum servo and two hydraulic circuits split front/rear with a pressure-relief valve in the rear circuit to prevent premature lockup of the back wheels. Bolt-on alloy wheels were provided, and had 6.5in (16.5cm) rims carrying 205/70 tyres — once more just like the 246.

Similarly, the chassis of the 308 is effectively an enlarged and modified version of the 246 chassis, an affair of oval and square-section steel tubes. This is built up above floor level at the front to support the suspension and at the rear for the same purpose as well as to frame the engine compartment and form a roll-over hoop. The steel body is directly welded to this tubular chassis.

Although near enough the same width as a 246, the 308GT4 is significantly bigger in all its other dimensions — for a start it's some 3in (7.6cm) taller. Apart from the extra length needed to house the additional rear seats, the 90deg bank angle of the V8 engine makes it take up more space longitudinally than the 65deg V6 had done. As a result the wheelbase is more than 8in (20.3cm) longer. Surprisingly, though, the car as a whole is only 2.6in (6.6cm) longer than the original Dino, partly because there is less front overhang and thus a smaller front boot only capable of housing a small space-saver spare wheel instead of a full-sized one. The rear boot, however — located behind the engine

just as for the 246 — is almost the same size. And with its bigger engine and extra seats the 308GT4 is inevitably heavier at around 25.3cwt (1,285kg) unladen but including oil, water and enough petrol for approximately 50 miles, compared to the 23.3cwt (1,183kg) of the 246 measured on the same basis.

Since this greater weight is carried on the same area of contact patch rubber as the first Dino's, the later car might be expected to have slightly lower cornering powers. But in compensation the 308GT4 is noticeably wider in track than the 246 — 1.9in (4.8cm) at the front and 1.6in (4cm) at the rear — and small increases in track confer disproportionately large improvements in roadholding.

REACTIONS

In addition to generating a good deal of enthusiasm, affection and respect, the 206/246 Dino undoubtedly created a trend. For by the time its successor, the 308GT4, appeared in the autumn of 1973 the Porsche 911S was no longer the only rival. Two other makers of prestige high performance cars had followed the Ferrari route by complementing their mainstream range of very fast cars with significantly less powerful 'junior' models. For Lamborghini the junior model was the Urraco with a 2.5-litre V8 engine developing 220bhp, compared to the 365bhp of the 3.9-litre V12 which powered the Jarama S. And both Ferrari and Lamborghini had accentuated the differences between their junior and senior models by introducing outrageously powerful 'supercar' models; the 380bhp Ferrari Berlinetta Boxer and the 440bhp Lamborghini Countach. Maserati could field no supercar of this calibre, but it had introduced a junior model in the form of the Merak with a (90deg) V6 engine developing 190bhp compared to the 330bhp of the Ghibli with its 4.7-litre V8.

The distinctive Dino 308GT4 badge which appeared on the earliest examples of the new car.

The rear seats of the 2+2 308GT4 made few concessions to comfort but at least answered one of the most common criticisms of the Dino 246.

It is to the credit of the 308GT4 that few journalists considered it outclassed by the two new models. Its engine, in particular, was highly praised. Paul Frère – as usual the first journalist to drive the car – described it as 'amazingly docile and flexible' in his test report of May 1974. He spoke of the ease with which other cars could be overtaken at high speeds on motorways, and squeezed out some pretty remarkable performance figures: 0–60mph (0–96.5kph) in 6.4 sec, 0–100mph (0–160kph) in 16.7sec and a top speed of 151.5mph (243kph) – not bad for a 'junior' model!

But he complained of excessive engine noise, an exceptionally poor steering lock and a heater with a difficult-to-control on/off action because it retained the old-fashioned water-valve form of control rather than the modern air-blending type. He found roadholding and handling of a very high order, yet somehow the 308GT4 lacked the precision and responsiveness of the 246 Dino.

These views were fully endorsed in the more lengthy full road test report which *Motor* published in January 1975 and which we reproduce here:

ROAD TEST
Ferrari Dino 308GT4
Reproduced from *Motor* 11 January 1975

FOR: *excellent performance, road holding and handling by normal standards; smooth torquey engine; powerful brakes*

AGAINST: *very poor fuel consumption, 'dead' steering; indifferent gearchange; poor lock; inefficient heating and non-existent face-level ventilation; poor finish.*

Nearly all Ferraris are classics but, even so, some are more memorable than others. The Dino 246GT was one of the memorable ones. That combination of stirring performance, almost unequalled handling and extreme beauty combined to produce not just a national hit, but a worldwide, all-time great, by which all subsequent GT cars have been judged. Inevitably, any car that now bears the name Dino must be compared with the 246 and if it proves impossible to measure its qualities in superlatives, then there will be no match.

Like Maserati and others Ferrari have given in to the demands of customers and the 308GT is their first mid-engined V8 2 plus 2.

In every other respect it is similar in concept to the 246. Its new all-alloy dohc engine is mounted across the frame ahead of and driving the rear wheels., The gearbox is the familiar five-speed Ferrari unit and the double wishbone suspension all round bears more than a passing resemblance to that of the old car.

The new engine is of three litres capacity and is a 90deg V8. It therefore demands more room longitudinally as well as laterally than the previous 65deg V6, and the body of the 308 is 2.6in longer than that of the 246. Like the Berlinetta Boxer's the body is built by Scaglietti, but the styling was done by Bertone rather than Pininfarina.

It is difficult to see how better use could have been made of the available space, but it is hard to treat the 'plus 2' with seriousness and those extra seats can only be considered of use for small children or extra luggage for there is no real space for adult legs.

Whatever body it might be clothed in, it is impossible to imagine a Ferrari without performance. Certainly the 308 is not lacking here, reaching 60mph in an impressive 6.4 seconds and 100mph in a mean of 16.7 secs. But it is from here on that it really impresses, bounding up to its maximum of over 150mph with astonishing rapidity. In tune with this exhilarating performance is the handling, which though perhaps lacking the precision and agility of the 246's is outstanding by ordinary standards. The brakes are powerful and reassuring and the ride remarkably smooth.

In other ways the new generation Dino disappoints. Its finish is indifferent for a car of this price: our test model suffered from a leaking floor, a sticking clutch, doors that dropped on their hinges and a light switch that failed after 3800 miles. Far more serious

than these niggling faults was the overall consumption, a hefty 14.1mpg and a tricky gearchange which was by far the worst of any Ferrari we have tried. The turning circle, too, is infuriatingly poor at around 40ft and the wheels rubbed on the wheel arches whenever the car was on full lock.

By absolute standards the 308 is in many respects a very fine car. But if you have been lucky enough to have sampled its predecessor (now, sadly, unobtainable) you might be faintly disappointed. We were.

Performance ⟦*****⟧

Though not startlingly different to the V6 unit of the original Dino, the 308's engine breaks new ground for Ferrari. Their eight-cylinder engines have been seen on the race track but this is the first time the configuration has been used in a Ferrari road car. It is also the first

Publicity material for the 308, typical of the period in its design and formulation.

Many features of the 246 interior were carried over into the 308.
The radio was sometimes mounted in the transmission tunnel.

time Ferrari has used toothed belts for the camshaft drives.

The alloy engine has a five-bearing crankshaft and eight cylinders set in a 90deg V. Toothed belts drive four overhead camshafts, two per bank, which in turn operate inclined valves via bucket tappets. The capacity of this oversquare unit is 2926 cc and its compression ratio is 8.8:1. Breathing is by four twin-choke 40DCNF Webers and ignition by twin Marello distributors.

Maximum power is 255bhp (DIN) and torque is a full 210ft lbs. The torque curve is beautifully flat and the engine will pull cleanly from as little as 1000rpm in fifth. Its 30–50mph time in this gear is in fact better than that of the 3.OCSi BMW in fourth, and vastly superior to that of the Maserati Merak and Lotus Elite.

Standing start accelerations are impressive partly because it is easy to spin the wheels despite the tail-heavy configuration. With the benefit of a wheelspin start we reached 60mph in an average of 6.4 seconds and 100mph in a mere 16.7 secs. These impressive times could undoubtedly have been bettered had the clutch pedal not tended to stick down during fast changes.

As the power keeps on coming right to the maximum of 7700rpm (and probably well beyond) the Dino is shatteringly quick over 100mph and will comfortably reach the red

Ferrari DINO 308 GT4 2+2

An early Ferrari publicity shot for the 308, the caption giving the model its full designation: 'Ferrari Dino 308GT4 2+2'.

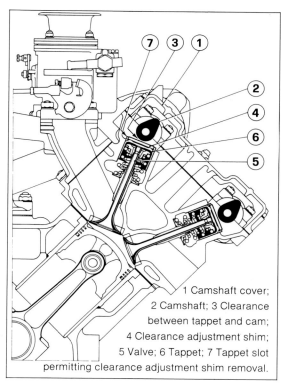

1 Camshaft cover; 2 Camshaft; 3 Clearance between tappet and cam; 4 Clearance adjustment shim; 5 Valve; 6 Tappet; 7 Tappet slot permitting clearance adjustment shim removal.

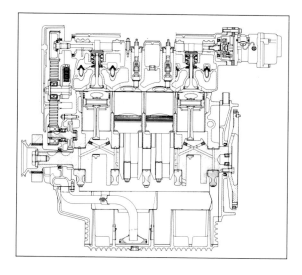

Longitudinal section through 308GT4 engine (above).

Combustion chamber and valvegear of 308GT4 engine (left).

line in top gear. Even allowing for an optimistic rev-counter this still gave a mean of around 152mph, some way off Ferrari's claim of 156mph. So easily does it attain such speeds that you frequently find yourself travelling 10–15mph faster than you realise.

Though a choke is supplied, starting of the Weber carburetted engine is best done in the traditional manner − with three or four pumps of the throttle. The engine warmed quickly and pulled cleanly almost immediately. Its sound is seldom harsh and its extreme smoothness throughout the rev range calls for a wary eye on the rev counter when pressing on through the gears.

Economy **

Our 14.1mpg overall fuel consumption can only be described as poor. It is slightly inferior to that of the heavier larger-engine Jaguar E-type, considerably worse than the consumptions of other more comparable machines like the Porsche Carrera and Lotus Elite. Even at a steady 30mph it recorded no better than 27.2mpg and by 100mph it had already fallen to 18.6mpg.

The car ran happily on four star fuel and will hold 17.2 gallons in its twin tanks. With a touring consumption of 18.7mpg the Dino has a range of some 320 miles between fill-ups.

A spread from a Ferrari publicity brochure for the Dino 308GT4.

Transmission ✳✳

Like the original Dino, the 308 has Ferrari's own five-speed gearbox which, together with the final drive, is mounted behind and beneath the transverse engine. A limited slip differential is included as standard.

The traditional Ferrari change features a slotted 'gate' with first back and to the left and the remaining four ratios spaced in the conventional 'H' pattern. Reverse is obtained by pressing the lever downwards, then to the left and forward. The gearchange on our test car was not like that of other Ferraris, though, being notchy and baulky and even lacking synchromesh. Hopefully, its faults were peculiar to this car.

Maranello-built boxes always need warming, but on this car the first to second movement remained awkward even when the oil was hot. All the gears were mildly obstructive and the synchromesh, particularly on fifth, proved weak. A heavy (42lb) long-travel clutch and forward positioning of the gearlever made fast changes difficult until you'd acquired the knack of perfect timing and co-ordination.

The ratios are rather low with first gear giving no more than 45mph. Second, third and fourth gears, are all quite close and at full bore top is engaged at little over 120mph. In practice, however, the extreme torque of the engine disguises any 'holes' and the car's ability to re-start on a 1 in 3 slope as easily as it pulls from 25mph in top proves there is little wrong with the chosen spacing.

CHASSIS

...ubular frame - Coupé 2+2 body ...esigned by Bertone - Front track 57.5 in - ...ear track 57.5 in - Length 169.3 in - ...idth 71 in - Height 46.5 in - Wheelbase ...0.4 in - Turning circle 492 in - ...eight 2536 lbs - 5-speed all synchromesh ...earbox, operated by central remote ...ntrol gear lever - Independent front and ...ar suspension - Limited-slip differential, ...corporated in the gearbox - ...ck and pinion steering - Servo ...sisted hydraulic brakes with ventilated ...scs on all four wheels; hand-brake on the ...ar wheels - Total capacity of the two ...ht-alloy fuel tanks 17.6 imp gal - ...el consumption 15/16 miles per imp gal - ...st light-alloy wheels; tyres size ...5/70 VR 14 X; special spare wheel ...th reduced section - Special wheels ...th Pirelli P7 tyres, on request - ...ectronic revolution counter and ...eedometer - Quartz clock - ...ats with headrest - Safety belts - ...ine fog lights - Electrically operated ...wer windows - Air conditioning ...d radio available as optional extras.

Handling ****

For their mid-engined cars, Ferrari opt for rack and pinion steering rather than the worm and peg systems of their front-engined models. Even so, the 308 suffers mildly from that dead feel found on the Daytona and some other Ferraris before it. For a sports car, it is also disappointingly low geared and the 3.25 turns required to swing from lock to lock would be 4.0 or more if the lock were not so extraordinarily poor. At low speeds it is very heavy, and parking the Dino is hard work for anybody. Once you are on the move though, the steering lightens considerably and is pleasant enough at high speed, despite the inherent lack of feel. Ruts and ridges cause the steering wheel to kick back violently in your hands, but most of the time it remains free of such irritation. The Dino is only mildly affected by crosswinds.

The 308's suspension is very similar to that of the preceding Dino; independent all round by unequal length wishbones, with coil springs and hydraulic dampers. Anti-roll bars are used front and rear.

There is quite strong initial understeer under power, followed on tighter corners by gradual transition to oversteer as more power is fed in. On faster bends increasing throttle causes the car to adopt a more neutral, stable attitude. Sudden lift-off results in nothing more than a slight tightening of line — just as it should be. Though the handling is hard to fault by normal standards we found the 308 lacked the feel and confidence-inspiring neutrality of the old 246.

Like the 246, the 308 comes on 6.5in Ferrari-made all-alloy rims, which are shod with Michelin XWX high-speed radials. Their cornering power in the dry is excellent, but on damp patches you soon learn to treat the throttle with extreme respect.

Brakes ****

High speeds demand powerful brakes and the Ferrari certainly has them. Servo assisted, ventilated disc brakes on all four corners arrest the car without effort from any speed and, more importantly, will do so repeatedly without drastic fade. At all times they retained their feel, though there was always a tendency to self-servo.

Our initial tests, carried out at only 30mph, showed how the pads need to be warmed for maximum efficiency. At this speed, a pressure of 25lb was required to give a 0.34g stop. In the fade test however, conducted at 98mph, 27lb was, initially, all that was required for a 0.5g deceleration. Six stops, though, were sufficient to cause very detectable fade and a consequent smell of cooking linings. The required pressure rose to 41lbs, but it remained at that level without further increases until the end of the test. The water splash had virtually no effect on braking efficiency.

The handbrake of our test car may well have required adjustment, for it failed to hold the car on a 1-in-3 slope even when placed on the last notch of its ratchet. In the same position it produced a 0.24g deceleration from 30mph. The legal requirement is 0.25g.

Accommodation ***

A 2 plus 2 the 308 may be, but only when the additional couple are children — and young ones at that. Entry to the back is straightforward enough, but adult-sized legs cannot be accommodated unless the front seats are pushed well forward — usually an impractical proposition. Even for children, the seat proved upright, hard and totally lacking in thigh support. Surprisingly, there is a reasonable degree of head room, though the head restraints like the seats, were definitely built with children in mind.

Front seat accommodation is far more generous and the uncluttered facia and console and hollow doors allow plenty of elbow room. Quite bulky oddments can be stored in the flip-back glovebox, the generous door pockets or handy little bins beside the rear seats. A further tray is located in their divide. More substantial items have to be

Motor Road Test 2/75 — Ferrari Dino 308GT4

PERFORMANCE

CONDITION

Weather	Dry; wind 0–18 mph
Temperature	38–42 F
Barometer	29.5 in Hg
Surface	Dry tarmac

MAXIMUM SPEEDS

	mph	kph
	See Text	
Terminal speeds:		
at ¼ mile	94	151
Speed in gears at (7700 rpm):		
1st	45	72
2nd	65	105
3rd	91	146
4th	123	198

ACCELERATION FROM REST

mph	sec	kph	sec
0–30	2.5		
0–40	3.4	0–40	2.0
0–50	5.1	0–60	3.1
0–60	6.4	0–80	5.0
0–70	8.7	0–100	7.0
0–80	10.3	0–120	9.3
0–90	13.7	0–140	12.5
0–100	16.7	0–160	16.7
Standing ¼	14.7		

ACCELERATION IN TOP

mph	sec	kph	sec
20–40			
30–50	7.9	60–80	4.4
40–60	7.2	80–100	4.8
50–70	7.2	100–120	4.2
60–80	6.9	120–140	4.5
70–90	7.1	140–160	5.0
80–100	8.2		

ACCELERATION IN 4th

mph	sec	kph	sec
20–40	5.9	40–60	3.2
30–50	5.1	60–80	3.1
40–60	4.8	80–100	2.9

50–70	4.6	100–120	2.8
60–80	4.6	120–140	3.2
70–90	4.8	140–160	3.5
80–100	5.6		

FUEL CONSUMPTION

Touring*	18.7 mpg	
	15.1 litres	100km
Overall	14.1 mpg	
	20.0 litres	100 km
Fuel grade	98 octane (RM)	
	4 star rating	
Tank capacity	17.2 galls	
	78.0 litres	
Max range	322 miles	
	518 km	
Test distance	1186 miles	
	1908 km	

* Consumption midway between 30 mph and maximum less 5 per cent for acceleration.

BRAKES

Pedal pressure deceleration and stopping distance from 30 mph (48 kph)

lb	kg	g	ft	m
25	11	0.34	88	27
50	23	0.68	44	13
75	34	0.87	34	10
100	45	1.00+	30	9
Handbrake		0.24	125	38

FADE

20½g stops at 1 min intervals from speed midway between 40 mph (64 khp) and maximum (97 mph 156 kph)

	lb	kg
Pedal force at start	27	12
Pedal force at 10th stop	48	22
Pedal force at 20th stop	45	20

STEERING

Turning circle between kerbs

	ft	m
left	39.4	12
right	40.2	12.3
Lock to lock	3.25 turns	
50ft ½ diam circle	1.3 turns	

CLUTCH

	in	cm
Free pedal movement	0.75	1.9
Additional to disengage	2.75	7.0
Maximum pedal load	42 lb	19 kg

SPEEDOMETER (mph)

Speedo	30	40	50	60	70	80	90	100
True mph	28	37	46	56	66	75	85	94

Distance recorder 3.2 per cent fast

WEIGHT

	cwt	kg
Unladen weight*	25.3	12.82
Weight as tested	29.0	14.71

* with fuel for approx 50 miles

Performance tests carried out by Motor's staff at the Motor Industry Research Association proving ground, Lindley.

Test Data: World copyright reserved; no reproduction in whole or in part without Editor's written permission.

housed in the rear luggage compartment which is located immediately behind the engine bay. We squeezed 5.0 cu ft. of our test luggage into its rectangular space. Yet more oddments can be laid around the space-saver tyre at the front of the car — cases, however, are out of the question. Five cu ft is in fact poor by any standards — less, in fact, than we found room for in the 246GT.

Ride Comfort ***

Though the Dino's ride is firm it is excellent for a car with such handling and cornering powers. It borders on the knobbly over really poor surfaces but is smooth enough on all other types of road. Though it never feels soft, neither is it harsh.

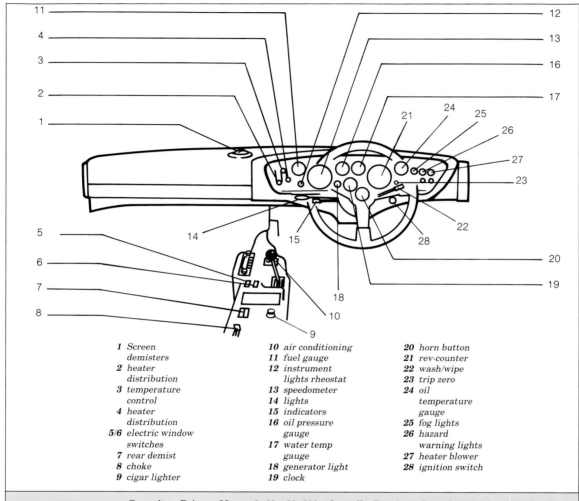

1	Screen demisters
2	heater distribution
3	temperature control
4	heater distribution
5/6	electric window switches
7	rear demist
8	choke
9	cigar lighter
10	air conditioning
11	fuel gauge
12	instrument lights rheostat
13	speedometer
14	lights
15	indicators
16	oil pressure gauge
17	water temp gauge
18	generator light
19	clock
20	horn button
21	rev-counter
22	wash/wipe
23	trip zero
24	oil temperature gauge
25	fog lights
26	hazard warning lights
27	heater blower
28	ignition switch

COMPARISONS	Capacity cc	Price £	Max mph	0–60 sec	30–50* sec	Overall mpg	Touring mpg	Length ft in		Width ft in		Weight cwt	Boot cu.ft
Ferrari Dino 308 GT	2927	8340	152†	6.4	7.9	14.1	18.7	14	1.3	5	7.3	25.3	5.0
Porsche Carrera	2687	9000	150†	5.5	**	16.7	–	14	1	5	3	21.2	4.3
Maserati Merak	2965	7821	140†	7.5	9.4	13.2	22.1	14	2	5	10	27.3	6.6
Jaguar E Type	5343	3743	146.0	6.4	6.0	14.5	–	15	4	5	6.75	28.8	3.8
Lotus Elite 502	1973	6255	125†	8.1	11.6	18.6	26.9	14	7.5	5	11.5	23.0	6.6
Jensen Interceptor	6276	8334	138.5	7.3	3.4	11.3	15.0	15	8	5	10	33.0	8.5
BMW 3.0 CSI	2985	7657	138	7.5	8.2	20.2	–	15	3.3	5	11	25.4	6.2
Alfa Romeo Montreal	2593	6085	135.2	8.1	8.8	13.8	–	13	10	5	5.8	25.1	3.2
Citroen SM EFI	2671	6691	142†	8.3	12.9	14.9	–	16	0.5	6	0.5	29.5	9.0

* *Kickdown for Jensen; top for other cars.*
† *Maker's claimed maximum on estimate.*
** *not recorded.*
– *Touring consumption not computed as fuel-injection prevented the measurement of steady speed consumption figures.*

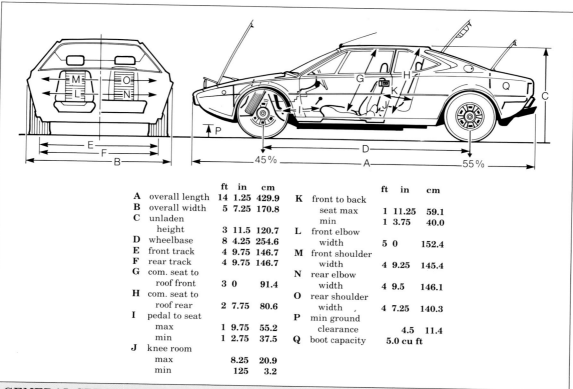

		ft	in	cm				ft	in	cm
A	overall length	14	1.25	429.9	**K**	front to back				
B	overall width	5	7.25	170.8		seat max	1	11.25	59.1
C	unladen					min	1	3.75	40.0
	height	3	11.5	120.7	**L**	front elbow			
D	wheelbase	8	4.25	254.6		width	5	0	152.4
E	front track	4	9.75	146.7	**M**	front shoulder			
F	rear track	4	9.75	146.7		width	4	9.25	145.4
G	com. seat to				**N**	rear elbow			
	roof front	3	0	91.4		width	4	9.5	146.1
H	com. seat to				**O**	rear shoulder			
	roof rear	2	7.75	80.6		width	4	7.25	140.3
I	pedal to seat				**P**	min ground			
	max	1	9.75	55.2		clearance		4.5	11.4
	min	1	2.75	37.5	**Q**	boot capacity	5.0 cu ft		
J	knee room								
	max		8.25	20.9					
	min		125	3.2					

GENERAL SPECIFICATION

ENGINE
Cylinders	V8
Capacity	2927 cc (178.6 cu in)
Bore/Stroke	81/71 mm (3.2/2.8 in)
Cooling	Water
Block	Light alloy
Head	Light alloy
Valves	dohc

Valve timing
inlet opens	34° btdc
inlet closes	46° abdc
ex opens	36° bbdc
ex closes	38° atdc
Compression	8.8:1
Carburetter	4 twin choke Weber 40 DCNF
Bearings	5 main
Fuel pump	Corona electric
Max power	255 bhp (DIN) at 7600 rpm
Max torque	209.8 lb ft (DIN) at 5000 rpm

TRANSMISSION
Type	5 speed manual
Clutch	Mechanically operated, sdp, diaphragm spring

Internal ratios and mph/1000 rpm
Top	0.952:1/21.0
4th	1.244:1/16.1
3rd	1.693:1/11.8
2nd	2.353:1/8.5
1st	3.418:1/5.8
Rev	3.247:1
Final drive	3.53:1 ratio

BODY/CHASSIS
Construction	Tubular steel frame

SUSPENSION
Front	Ind by wishbones, coils and anti-roll bar
Rear	Ind by wishbones, coils and anti-roll bar

STEERING
Type	Rack and pinion
Assistance	None
Toe-in	0.08–0.157 in
Camber	0°-10′–0°-30′
Castor	4°
King pin	9°-30′

BRAKES
Type	Disc all round
Servo	Yes
Circuit	Divided front/rear
Rear valve	Yes
Adjustment	Automatic on all four wheels

WHEELS
Type	Ferrari light alloy 14×6.5 in
Tyres	Michelin 205/70 VR14 XWX; Spare, Michelin 105 R18X
Pressures	To 95 mph F26; R29; over 130 mph F31; R37; Spare, 21

ELECTRICAL
Battery	12 volt, 66 ah
Polarity	Negative earth
Generator	Alternator
Fuses	18
Headlights	4×55W Halogen

STANDARD EQUIPMENT

Adjustable steering	No	Head restraints	Yes	Parcel shelf	No
Anti-lock brakes	No	Heated rear window	No	Petrol filler lock	No
Armrests	No	Laminated screen	Yes	Radio	No
Ashtrays	Yes	Lights		Rev counter	Yes
Breakaway mirror	Yes	Boot	No	Seat belts	
Cigar lighter	Yes	Courtesy	Yes	Front	Yes
Childproof locks	No	Engine bay	Yes	Rear	Yes
Clock	Yes	Hazard warning	Yes	Seat recline	Yes
Coat hooks	No	Map reading	No	Seat height adjuster	No
Dual circuit brakes	Yes	Parking	No	Sliding roof	No
Electric windows	No	Reversing	Yes	Tinted glass	No
Energy absorb steering col	Yes	Fog	Yes	Combination wash/wipe	Yes
Fresh air ventilation	No	Locker	Yes	Wipe delay	No
Grab handles	No	Outside mirror	Yes	Vanity mirror	Yes

IN SERVICE

GUARANTEE

Duration .... **1 year or 10,000 miles**

MAINTENANCE

Schedule .... **Every 3000 miles**
Free service ..... **At 600, 1200 miles**
Labour for year ...... **Approx £220**

DO-IT-YOURSELF

Sump	**16.0 pints, SAE 10W50**
Gearbox/	
Differential	**0.88 pints, SAE 90**
Steering gear	**0.35 pints, SAE 90**
Coolant	**31.6 pints**
Chassis lubrication	
Contact breaker gap	**0.012–0.15**
Spark plug type	**Champion N6Y**
Spark plug gap	**0.020–0.024**
Tappets (cold)	
inlet	**0.008–0.010**
exhaust	**0.012–0.014**

REPLACEMENT COSTS

Brake pads (front)	**£7.19**
Clutch unit	**£36.35**
Complete exhaust system	**£149.50**
Engine (new)	**£4250.00**
Damper (front)	**£18.50**
Front wing	**£69.00**
Gearbox (new)	**£2350.00**
Oil filter	**£6.91**
Starter motor	**approx £106**
Windscreen	**£114.08**

Make: Ferrari
Model: Dino 308GT4
Makers: Ferrari Automobili SpA SEFAC, casella postale 589, 41100 Modena, Italy
Concessionaires: Maranello Concessionaires Ltd, Egham by-pass, Surrey
Price: £7128.00 plus £594.0 car tax plus £617.76 VAT equals £8339.76. Electric windows, £114.66; Leather/cloth interior, £253.89; Air conditioning, £374.40; heated rear window, £30.42 gives total as tested of £9113.13

At the wheel ***

Unlike some other Italian companies Ferrari are reasonably adept at building their cockpits to accommodate people of various shapes and sizes. There is a hint of the long-armed short-legged Italianate character about the driving position but this can be virtually eliminated by careful positioning of the reclining seats. Far more disconcerting to most of our testers were the heavily offset pedals, the heavy, long travel clutch being particularly awkward – though we discovered after a time that clean changes could be made with only a short stab on the clutch.

The remaining controls are well positioned with three stalks looking after most of the minor facilities. The larger of the left-hand ones is a compound light switch operating side-lamps, and the automatic pop-up headlamps as well as main beam and the flash for the fog lights. A smaller one in front controls the indicators. The remaining one to the right of the column works the powerful electric washers and two-speed wipers. To the right of the facia, angled towards the driver, are a row of toggle switches and associated warning lights which together take care of the blower fan, and hazard warning and driving lights. The potent air horns are worked by the 'Dino' button in the centre of the leather-covered Momo steering wheel and the controls for the electric windows, heated rear screen and redundant choke are on the console.

All our testers complained about the Klippan seat belts which are particularly awkward to adjust, the tensioner being on the diagonal rather than the lap strap, and which, far worse, tend to slip off the shoulder in use.

The driver's seat is of the reclining bucket type and offers excellent support to all key areas of the body. Both the thigh and lumbar regions are comfortably located and a well-curved back-rest ensures good lateral support. A handy footrest is built into the edge of the console.

Several drivers complained that the heater and ignition switches were awkward to reach when they were belted in. Another found reverse gear hard to engage for the same reason.

Visibility ****

Poor visibility is a failing of many mid-engined designs and has made some a dubious pleasure for road use. Though open to improvement the 308 is an exception. The slope of the nose, however, puts it just out of sight from the driving seat, despite the high, forward seating position. Rearward vision ends with the far edge of the engine cover as far as reversing is concerned, so one has to memorise the remaining length of stubby tail.

But the thickish rear pillars aren't as obstructive as one might imagine though their painted inner surfaces do cause reflections in bright sunlight. Due to its sheltered position, the rear screen never required wiping or use of the heated element. A good wiper pattern results in no real blind spots of the front screen either and the wipers seemed to work well at speeds much in excess of 100mph. The headlights were no more than adequate on dipped beam, but impressive with all four in action.

Instruments ***

Ferrari owners no doubt expect a full array of instruments. The Dino has a more than adequate selection which includes a matching speedometer and rev-counter sandwiching a trio of smaller dials in the form of oil pressure and water temperature gauges and a clock. Completing the layout are yet more gauges for oil temperature and fuel. Though impressive in quantity, the instrumentation is far from perfect. The dials are all on the small side and the calibrations of both speedometer and rev-counter unnecessarily mean. As the outer gauges are frequently obscured by the rim of the steering wheel, we feel it would make more sense to locate one of them, probably the oil temperature gauge, where the less vital clock is. Subtle, rheostat-controlled green lighting illuminates the cluster at night. Both a trip and total mileage recorder are included in the speedometer head.

Heating **

The heating system is inadequate and suffers from several major faults. First, it is of the old-fashioned water mix type and is therefore slow to react to changes of adjustment and is very inconsistent in its operation. Secondly, the distribution, with its separate controls for left and right, allows either full flow to the screen or air split between screen and floor — never full flow to the floor. In consequence, the volume of air to the footwells is frequently insufficient. Even the noisy, single speed fan does little to remedy matters.

Ventilation *

Other than by aiming cold air from the three screen outlets, the Dino has no ventilation system. The alternative to opening windows — a sorry state of affairs in this class of car — is the purchase of the optional air-conditioning unit. This was fitted to our test car and works well, though the lack of face level vents means the air is still poorly distributed.

Noise ***

A Ferrari would not be a Ferrari unless the music of the motore was dominant. Even though it is sited well behind the driver's ears, the uncharacteristic purr of the Dino's

The clean, uncluttered lines of the 308GT4

high-revving V8 is always with you. Unlike the chain driven V12 units the Dino's belt-driven cams do not jangle and clatter and the sound is merely the complete one of the busy and potent all-alloy engine. Induction noise is high and the gasp of the twin-choke Webers, through their intake on the rear quarters which is noticeable with closed windows, becomes obtrusive when driving with them open. Road noise is commendably low and wind roar, which is quite perceptible at 80mph, rises surprisingly little with speed and is only marginally worse at 150mph.

Finish **

Ferrari's 'baby' car is a strange mixture of the quality coachbuilt vehicle and low volume 'special'. The doors dropped on their hinges, the interior handles (easily mistaken for ashtrays) had sharp edges and the facia trim didn't fit properly. Even the door mouldings with their projecting screw heads smacked of the kitcar market. In contrast, the neatly trimmed Momo steering wheel and beautifully upholstered seats did project the sort of image one would expect of a car costing £8,340. Still more impressive is the finish on the Bertone body which is protected by rubber inserts in the full-width bumpers and enhanced by the familiar Ferrari alloy wheels first seen on the 246GT. The boot is trimmed in coarse-weave material which assists in keeping luggage fixed under hard driving conditions.

Though the brakes were little affected by our customary water splash test, the body was, and a good gallon of water was mopped from the mats afterwards.

Equipment ***

The Ferrari's equipment is sparse for an expensive car. If, however, you believe that one buys a Ferrari solely for its performance and are happy to add the extras yourself, then you will most probably be satisfied with the basic article plus a handful of options. It comes with a five-speed gearbox, full instrumentation, reversing, fog and hazard warning lights,

courtesy and engine lights, head restraints, seat belts front and rear and air horns.

Obvious omissions include face level ventilation, the only alternative to which is full air-conditioning at £374.40, and a heated rear window which is also available for an extra £30.42. The electric windows cost £114.66 and a mixture of leather and cloth trim is a further £253.89. All leather is a full £301.86. Even the radio is extra.

In service

The engine compartment is opened by a lever set into the driver's door pillar. It is alongside that for the boot and the pair can be locked in position. The bonnet is self-propping and tilts forward to reveal a pretty full compartment, dominated by the large black crackle-finish air filter. Access to the rearward bank of plugs is good, as it is to the oil filter, both

The characteristic Ferrari circular tail-lamps remained a feature on the 308.

distributors and the quartet of Webers (once the air-filter is removed). Working on the forward bank, however, does not look so easy.

The bootlid opens the same way, and hides a most comprehensive tool kit, jack and spare set of drive belts for the engine. The bootlid has a catch at each corner and one usually has to apply a little weight to each side when closing. For the same reason, a good pull is required on the release for the front compartment, the lever for which is found under the facia on the driver's side. Under the self-propping lid are four distinct sections, the first of which is solely for the exit of air from the radiator. Behind that sits the spacesaver spare tyre which is said to be safe to speeds of around 95mph. To its left are the controls for one set of pop-up headlamps as well as the washer bottle and compressor for the air horns. The other side houses the battery and the other set of headlamps. The lockable glovebox contains a comprehensive, leather-wrapped handbook and a well labelled bank of fuses.

IN PRODUCTION

Since the 246 Dino system of chassis numbering was simply extended for the 308GT4, and since there was also an overlap period during which both models were being produced, there is some doubt not merely about the exact number of cars that were made but also about the last chassis number of one and the first of the other. According to the *Ferrari Register* compiled by Robert Abraham the first chassis number was 07202 and sole production of the 308GT4 started at 08520, finishing at 15604. But according to *A Guide to Ferrari Cars Since 1959,* published by Maranello Concessionaires Ltd and based on (not always accurate) factory information, the first 308GT4 chassis number was 08354 and the last was 15474.

If the factory records are accepted, 2,826

308GT4s were built altogether, from the start of production in 1974 to its finish in 1980 — barely three-quarters of the 3,883 206/246 Dinos which are said to have been made during a production run of roughly similar length. On that basis the 308GT4 was a failure, but it must be remembered that it appeared in the depths of the Energy Crisis, when motoring in almost every country of the world was all but paralysed by emergency speed limits and queues at filling stations. At that time ordinary cars were difficult to sell; high-performance cars could hardly be given away.

Undeterred by all this, Luigi Chinetti through his NART team entered a highly modified 308GT4 as a Group 5 car in the 1974 Le Mans race with an engine developing 300bhp at 8,200rpm. However it retired early in the race with clutch problems. It was at Le Mans again in 1975, but was withdrawn by Luigi Chinetti, along with the other NART cars, following a dispute with the race organisers.

Thus the episode brought no glory to the car, and its sales were also adversely influenced by the introduction in 1976, covered later in this chapter, of the 308GTB. This two-seater car styled by Pininfarina was immediately seen as the true successor to the 246 Dino.

On top of all this, the criticisms of the 308GT4's fuel consumption, finish, steering lock, and heating and ventilation can hardly have contributed to its success. Many customers, however, offset some of the weaknesses of the heating and ventilation system by having the optional air conditioning system fitted (£374.40 extra in 1975). A much smaller number expressed their opinion of the occasional rear seats by replacing them with another optional extra; a rear luggage platform fitted with straps to retain cases in position.

It was perhaps because the Dino name had lost its charisma and sales were flagging that in 1976 the addition of 'Ferrari' badges to the car were authorised. From then on the car was badged both as a 308GT4 and as a Ferrari.

THE 208GT4

Yet the record was not wholly one of failure, since potential demand for the 308GT4 in Italy was enough to stimulate the creation of a special home-market model. This was the 208GT4 introduced at the Geneva Show of March 1975. It was designed to take advantage of an Italian tax concession by being fitted with a 2-litre version of the V8 engine. With an output of only 170bhp at 7,700rpm, the 208 was considerably slower than the 255bhp standard car. Nevertheless, some 840 of these cars were made.

THE 308GTB

Just before the Paris Show of October 1975 came a trickle of information about a new and exciting Ferrari, the 308GTB. The trickle soon turned into a flood and the new car – a proper two-seater this time – was at once welcomed as the true successor to the 246 Dino. To begin with, *aficionados* warmly approved Ferrari's decision to return to Pininfarina for its styling. (Poor Bertone, responsible for many beautiful body designs over the years, most unfairly gained little credit from their brief association with Ferrari – until years later when the merits of their 308GT4 began to be appreciated.)

Equally warmly approved was the result of Pininfarina's efforts. Although the new body was far crisper and more modern, it bore more than a passing resemblance to the 246 Dino's. In particular, it had inherited the air scoops in the flanks and a certain similarity about the curvature of the front wheelarches. The rear buttresses had been retained, too, with a gentle reverse curvature to the rear screen.

In its general layout and principal mechanical components the 308GTB was very similar to the 308GT4, with double wishbone suspension all round and the same transversely-orientated 255bhp V8 engine mounted behind the driver but ahead of the rear wheels driving through a five-speed transaxle. By returning to the 246 theme, though, and dispensing with occasional rear seats, the GTB was shorter and lighter than the GT4.

There were, moreover, some further differences. The engine had dry sump (to begin with) rather than wet sump lubrication, for instance, and the body was made of glass fibre – the first to be constructed of this material by Ferrari. At the time the quality of the glass fibre body panels and their freedom from distortion or ripple was highly praised, but Ferrari were to revert to steel for a body material later in the car's production run.

The final difference was symbolic: the 308GTB was always badged as a Ferrari, not as a Dino. In a way the change in philosophy amounted to an admission that the smaller Ferraris did just as much honour to the marque – if not more – than the bigger ones. But the 308GTB nevertheless marks the end of the Dino era, so its further progress lies beyond the scope of this book.

7 Afterthoughts: the Lancia Stratos

Although the original Dino was seldom raced or rallied in its day, it nevertheless managed to achieve a long and honourable competition career at one remove. Five years after the 246 had gone out of production, its engine still lived on and was winning major rallies in the Lancia Stratos.

Like the Dino itself, this famous competition car came into being through a complex web of interacting circumstances. The first strand of the story comes from the world of the concept car or styling exercise. While body design involves many fundamental engineering requirements — adequate torsional stiffness, sound ergonomics, good aerodynamic performance, proper safety protection and so on — there is a sense in which the major styling studios are in the fashion business: fashion in metal. When Pininfarina or Ital Design introduce some striking new creation at the Turin Show, their objective is far more to prove their continuing ability to combine aesthetic balance with visual innovation than to create cars which will actually go into production — though they often hope they will. The result is frequently a design which is wildly extravagant and totally impractical. In fact very few concept cars have ever been directly translated into products which the public can buy (the Lotus Esprit is one of the rare exceptions) though some details such as the shape of a window or the curve of a waistline are often to be seen on production models a year or two later.

Even by the standards of the fashion industry, however, the styling exercise which Bertone displayed at the Turin Show of November 1970 was pretty extreme. During its development Bertone had been contemplating using the names Stratos and Ionos — meaning from the stratosphere or ionosphere — for a range of skis they were developing. But when the project was dropped the name Stratos proved just right for their latest automotive creation: it very accurately expressed the character of what was in essence a futuristic fantasy. Some hint of the impact made by this fantasy is to be found in the following extract from the author's own report on that particular Turin Show:

'Perhaps the most outrageous of this year's confections was the Bertone Stratos, aptly and cynically described by our artist Brian Hatton as the "lie of the century". To achieve the recumbent position implied by the pun the intrepid motorist is expected to step straight into the cockpit of this two-seater via a doormat let into the thin end of the wedge which the whole car constitutes. Once settled into his low-slung seat he pulls back the steering wheel into the operating position, an action which through a system of mechanical links causes the nearly horizontal windscreen/door to lower itself over him. Steering complexities are minimised by using a rack and pinion unit which is pivoted about its own axis; similar arrangements have been used in cars from time immemorial to allow easy adjustment of the column rake.'

'Set into the deeply recessed side panels are windows which not only allow the driver to look sideways, but also, under a thin, nearly horizontal divider, to subject the ground near him, Marzal style, to a close inspection. Mirrors are built into the recess just forward of the upper side window though some direct rearward vision is possible, while beside the driver is an instrument panel obscured by a graticule stolen from the oscilloscope of the nearest diagnostic centre. All this is propelled by a Lancia Fulvia 1.6 HF engine and transmission mounted behind the driver but ahead of the rear wheels, Fiat-type MacPherson struts being used at the front. Access to the engine is via an enormous V-shaped grid, hinged at one side, which constitutes the major styling motif of the car.'

This brief description by no means exhausted the catalogue of novelties. Engine cooling air, for example, was drawn in through vee slats in that hinged grid and exhausted by electric fans through a radiator in the back panel. Lighting was by an array of ten rectangular lamps mounted in the tip of the wedge, with a similar arrangement in what was described as a 'labial strip' at the rear. In the year of The Wedge the Stratos was King.

But that it was also an exercise in pure fantasy was emphasised by another Bertone creation, also exhibited at the 1970 Turin Show: the body of the new Lamborghini P250 Urraco. It was almost as striking in appearance as the Stratos, but entirely practical (though a sham 2 + 2 like the 308GT4).

Bertone, however, didn't acknowledge the impracticality of the Stratos, and to its credit it was at least driven quite extensively on the road – unlike many styling exercises which are often non-running mock-ups. Some journalists were even invited to try the car

and were said to have found it easy to drive, but – surprise, surprise – difficult to get in and out of. There is a suspicion, though, that those who did manage to get into the car and then drive it must have been built like jockeys – and flat-racing jockeys at that.

Fortunately for Bertone, at least one important figure of the Italian motoring establishment took the project more seriously. This was Cesare Fiorio, Lancia's competition manager who at that time was faced with a challenge and an opportunity. The challenge was to find a replacement for Lancia's principal rallying weapon which had been highly successful for several years. This was the lightweight HF (High Fidelity) version of the front-wheel drive Fulvia coupe with its unusual engine, distinguished by a narrow-angle V4 layout that Lancia had pioneered in the twenties. But expanded to a capacity of 1.6 litres giving around 135bhp in rally form, this engine had reached the limit of its development, whereas the Alpine-Renaults which were beginning to outclass the Fulvia had some 170bhp at their disposal, while Porsche 911s were endowed with more than 200bhp.

In addition, the world of rallying was moving away from front-engined or front-wheel drive cars. Not only were the rear-engined Alpine-Renaults and Porsche 911s proving a powerful threat, but all the designers of Grand Prix and sports-racing cars had changed over to the mid-engined configuration. To a top-class rally driver mid-engined and rear-engined cars have certain advantages. They're easily induced to take up the tail-out 'sideways' attitude in bends which is essential to fast yet controllable cornering on loose surfaces. The large, opposite-lock angle of drift makes high speeds possible but at the same time can be controlled to speed the car up or slow it down in a corner which the driver may never have encountered before. Cesare Fiorio sought the views of his team on these matters and received a unanimous opinion that a

LANCIA STRATOS
PROTOTIPO 1970

*The outrageous design of the Bertone Stratos prototype provoked
mixed reactions at the car's unveiling in Turin in 1970.*

powerful mid-engined car with a low polar
moment of inertia (see page 47) and a
short wheelbase was essential to future
success.

So much for the challenge. The opportunity
sprang from the guaranteed and stable
financial future that Lancia had gained
through its acquisition, a year before in
October 1969, by Fiat. A few months before
that, of course, Ferrari had similarly come
under Fiat control, bringing with it a valuable source of engines and other components,
as well as competition expertise, into the
group. Furthermore, *Ingegnere* Ugo Gobbato,
who had been working for Ferrari, had
recently also been appointed managing
director of Lancia.

One of Cesare Fiorio's first thoughts was to
consider the 246 as a possible replacement for
the Fulvia HF coupe. The Lancia competi-
titions department did in fact prepare a Dino
for Sandro Munari in the Tour de France, but
the car never competed. It was considered too
heavy and too long in the wheelbase to have
the long-term potential needed. The Dino's
tubular chassis, too, looked vulnerable to the
tremendous pounding inseparable from
modern rallying.

When the Bertone Stratos came along,
however, Fiorio was undeterred by its
impracticalities and extravagances of styling
and quickly saw it as a possible basis for a
compact and lightweight mid-engined rally
car of great potential. A meeting was

**LANCIA STRATOS
PROTOTIPO 1970**

The space-age rear end of the Bertone Stratos concept car.

convened at Lancia's competition head-quarters attended by Cesare Fiorio, Ugo Gobbato, Nuccio Bertone, and, of course, the car itself. The first step was to turn the Stratos into something more practical. It needed a pair of ordinary doors, greater ground clearance and must be both taller and shorter. The second step was to find a more powerful engine.

Bertone, and his chief stylist at that time, Marcello Gandini, accepted the task of reshaping the car completely, while Gobbato and Fiorio pondered the question of the engine. The Flavia 2000 boxer unit in turbocharged form, the Fiat 130 V6 and the Fiat Dino V6 engines were all considered, but the final decision was for the Ferrari version of the 2.4-litre V6 with which the

Lancia competitions department were already familiar through their earlier assessment exercise. Lancia engineer Gianni Tonti was set to work on the mechanical design, helped on a consultancy basis by the well-known Giampaolo Dallara, formerly technical director of Lamborghini.

REALISATION

The Lancia HF Stratos which resulted from all these second thoughts appeared a year later at the Turin Show of 1971. A mid-engined car powered by the 246 Dino engine and transmission, it shared a familial resemblance with the previous car, but not much else apart from the wheelbase and track.

Those characteristics alone, however, were enough to make it extremely unusual. There is no 'ideal' or 'correct' ratio of wheelbase to track, but commonsense suggests, and experience confirms, that lengthening wheelbase in relation to track improves straight-line high-speed directional stability at the expense of steering response in corners, while shortening the wheelbase in relation to track improves steering response in corners at the expense of directional stability. For decades racing teams have been fielding long-wheelbase cars for high-speed circuits such as Spa and short-wheelbase cars for twisty circuits such as Monaco, but the definitions of long and short are here a matter of judgement, not scientific calculation. The Stratos, though, must have been one of the 'squarest' cars ever built, with a ratio of wheelbase to track of only 1.50, compared to 1.64 for the Dino, itself pretty short in the wheelbase. For a typical modern front-wheel drive hatchback like a Volkswagen Golf, the ratio is around 1.75.

But in all other respects the Lancia HF Stratos was fundamentally different from the Bertone Stratos which preceded it. To start with it was essentially a conventional three-box shape with a pair of ordinary front-hinged doors instead of a one-piece wedge entered from the front. The near prone Formula 1 type of driving position had been abandoned in favour of a more sensible and upright seating arrangement in a more roomy cockpit. There was no space behind the seats and the whole of the front boot was taken up with the footwells, spare wheel, radiator and other components, but a short, deep luggage boot ran across the tail of the car behind the engine, and large trays were built into the doors to carry crash helmets. No window-winding mechanisms were fitted; instead the glasses in the doors moved up and down in an arc from a forward pivot point with a simple friction locking mechanism to hold them in any desired position.

But the functional character of the new car did not prevent the stylists from making their statements in a number of ways, particularly the very steeply raked wind

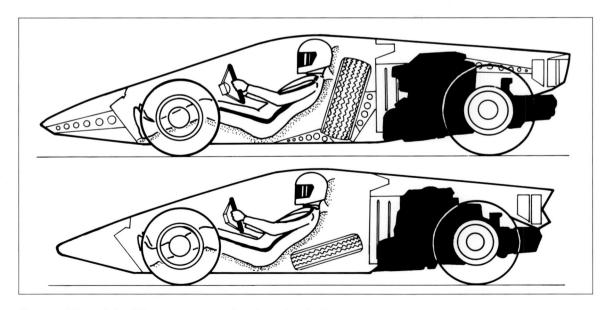

Copies of the original Bertone concept drawings for the Stratos, demonstrating the extraordinary seating position of the driver.

The Lancia HF Stratos was the eventual outcome of Bertone's futuristic styling exercise, but it bore little relation to the original Stratos design.

screen which was brought round in a wide sweep to a pair of unusually slender pillars, the doors having frameless windows. Horizontal slats allowed air to escape from the engine compartment and permitted some measure of rearward visibility through the small window at the back of the cockpit. These slats, together with the tail, boot and rear wheelarches, formed part of a one-piece cover which could be lifted to expose the engine and rear suspension; the bonnet at the front of the car was a similar large hinged moulding. Ordinary circular rear lamps were mounted in the cut-off tail, while at the front was a battery of pop-up headlamps and driving lights.

Maximum strength, minimum weight and ease of servicing and repair were the criteria governing the structure of the car. In place of the tubular type of chassis favoured by Ferrari for both the 206/246 and 308GT4 Dinos, Lancia and Bertone followed the best competition practices of the day and gave the Stratos a high-efficiency lightweight steel monocoque structure. This was very largely composed of a small, closed, central 'tub' in which the driver and co-driver sat. Box-section steel outriggers extended forwards from it, however, to support the radiator and front suspension. Similarly, a further structure of box-section beams extended downwards and rearwards from the aft bulkhead to provide mounting points for the rear suspension and to support the engine. The exceptionally slender screen pillars were only able to give modest support to the roof, so the rear bulkhead was reinforced with a substantial tubular rollover bar. The bonnet and engine cover were both lightweight glass fibre mouldings.

Double wishbone suspension was initially fitted at both ends of the car, with coil springs, telescopic dampers, and anti-roll bars. Rack and pinion steering was used, and many parts from other models in the group such as the Fiat 124 and X1/9 were incorporated in the car. Massive ventilated disc brakes for all four wheels completed the running gear, no servo being used to actuate them due to the lightness of the car.

Everything was designed for the car's role in rallying and sportscar racing, which meant that the wheelarches had to be able to accept without alteration wheels and tyres of widely differing sizes, and that it must be possible to remove and replace all the mechanical components very quickly. The suspension was fully adjustable, the ride height could be varied by 1.5in (3.5cm) and both front and rear anti-roll bars had three different settings available. The back cover could quickly be taken off by undoing four bolts and unplugging the rear wiring harness, while a removable cross-member allowed easy withdrawal of the complete engine/transmission assembly.

The Dino's integral transaxle, bolted to the sump of the engine, didn't meet the criteria for quick changes of the final drive gears, so the adoption of a longitudinal orientation for the power unit, allowing a separate, more accessible gearbox mounted behind it, was at one stage considered. But the possibility was rejected on the grounds of cost, and the disadvantage of the transmission layout accepted. In practice the time for changing the final drive gears between special stages was finally reduced to a best of about twenty minutes.

But the transversely orientated V6 power unit and the five-speed transaxle of the 246 Dino were retained only in basic form, the engine, particularly, being subjected to an extensive tuning and modification programme. One of the first problems to be attacked was the inherent hesitation when cornering hard due to fuel surge in the carburetters under the influence of lateral acceleration. Fuel injection was considered as a solution but rejected, again on the grounds of cost, and instead the float chambers of the three Weber carburetters were relocated to eliminate the problem. With 48mm instead of 40mm chokes, these carburetters were considerably bigger than those of the standard engine, and in conjunction with many other detail modifications helped to increase the power output. For the standard road-going cars this was always quoted as 190bhp at 7,000rpm compared to 195bhp at 7,600rpm for the 246 Dino, even though the considerably less constricted exhaust system of the Stratos suggests a higher output. It was rumoured that Ferrari only allowed Lancia to use the engine on condition that a lower power figure was quoted. But the engines of the works cars were developing 250bhp or more from the early stages of the project.

The net result of all these labours was a

formidable car. It was small, being about the same width as a Dino, but more than 21in (52.5cm) shorter. And with that diminutive size went a low weight of just under one ton (1,000kg) and thus an extremely healthy power/weight ratio.

EVOLUTION

The basic development work took about a year to complete, so the Lancia Stratos did not make its first appearance in competition until the Tour de Corse of November 1972. At the wheel was Sandro Munari — who was to become one of the car's most successful drivers — with beside him his usual co-driver, Mario Mannucci. The event was not a great success, the car being forced to retire due to suspension problems. A month later, in the Rally Costa del Sol with the same driver and co-driver, the car was again forced to retire and for the same reason.

The problem was that the inherently twitchy behaviour of the car was being compounded by changes from strong understeer to pronounced oversteer so sudden and so unpredictable that even a highly talented driver couldn't tame them. On surfaced roads some sort of control could just be retained, but on the loose gravel of rally special sections the car became virtually unmanageable. The defect was eventually discovered to have two causes, the first of which was deflection of the steering arms under load.

This was easily cured, but the second fault, a similar deflection in the rear suspension proved more troublesome. A complete redesign of the system became necessary, the double-wishbone arrangement being discarded in favour of a MacPherson strut, location of the bottom of the hub carrier being provided by a reversed rear wishbone and a long fore-and-aft reaction rod running forwards to a pivot point ahead of the engine. With these faults corrected, the Stratos

rapidly began to establish itself as one of the fastest and most successful rally cars ever created. But it always remained a nervous machine, highly sensitive to throttle openings in a corner, which demanded a driver of high ability to exploit its power and response. In less skilled hands it could be lethal.

But there was no shortage of driving talent, and the Stratos embarked on a record-breaking series of wins. The first was in the Spanish Firestone Rally of April 1973, again driven by Munari and Mannucci. A few weeks later, driven once more by Munari but with Jean-Claude Andruet as co-driver, this was followed by a highly creditable second place as a GT racer in the Targa Florio, with lap times that were surprisingly close to those of much more powerful cars such as the Ferrari 312P. Wins in the Tour de l'Aisne and the Tour de France came later in the year.

Towards the end of the season the Lancia rally team was reinforced by the arrival of the well-known English engineer and driver, Mike Parkes, another former Ferrari employee. He set to work developing a more powerful four-valve version of the engine and also organised a turbocharging development programme.

At about the same time Bertone and Lancia began to build the 500 cars needed if the Stratos were to graduate from being a sports prototype to homologation as a Group 4 GT Special. The steel monocoque and glass fibre body panels were manufactured at Bertone's Grugliasco factory, while final assembly took place at Lancia's Chivasso works. All cars had left-hand drive and were identical in basic design to the works cars with fully adjustable suspension, but these production models were fitted with the standard 190bhp engine.

The following year, 1974, started badly. The energy crisis was in full swing and the Monte Carlo Rally was cancelled. But then the 24-valve engine, developing around

The Stratos was developed into one of the greatest rally cars of all time. This is the car which won the World Rally Championship in 1973.

300bhp, was deemed ready for competition and two cars powered by it were entered for the Targa Florio. The Munari-Andruet car led at first but was forced to drop out because of fuel feed problems. Happily the Larrousse and Ballestrieri car took over the lead and went on to win the race.

Completion of the required minimum of 500 cars took longer than expected, however, but was finally certified on 1 October by the internationally respected engineer and journalist, Paul Frère, already mentioned in these pages, acting as a consultant to the sport's controlling body, the FIA. All the cars ever built were made in this single production batch, and some writers were later to doubt that the agreed minimum were in fact produced. The consensus of informed opinion today, though, is that a little more than 500 cars – perhaps 540 – were produced altogether. Very few of these were bought purely as road-going 'homologation specials', most being used or intended for competition of one sort or another.

SUCCESS

The pressure then lifted, the rally season was reinstated and during October and

Lancia and Ferrari in motorsport

When Lancia and Ferrari co-operated to create the Stratos, it was not the first time the two companies had been linked together in a competition programme. A much earlier association had developed in Grand Prix racing during the middle fifties.

This had its roots a few years earlier when Lancia decided to enter Grand Prix racing for the first time. Despite being in acute financial difficulties, they commissioned the brilliant engineer Vittorio Jano – the same man who was later to design the Dino engine for Ferrari – to create a completely new Formula 1 car for them in conditions of considerable secrecy. At that time the formula required 2.5-litre unsupercharged or 750cc supercharged engines, but beyond these constraints Jano had total freedom to design. In some ways the Lancia D50 he created was conventional in design for the day, being a front-engined/rear-wheel drive car with double-wishbone suspension at the front and a de Dion rear axle. Yet in many respects it was also ahead of its time, for it was one of the first designs to consider the value of a low polar moment of inertia (see page 47) for improved responsiveness in corners – as well as a short wheelbase – and one of the first to use the engine as a stressed chassis member. That engine, a four-camshaft 2,487cc V8, formed one of the car's three main structural elements. A small spaceframe extended forwards from it to support the radiator, part of the front suspension and other components, while a larger spaceframe extended rearwards to carry the driver and support the rear suspension and a rear transaxle.

The engine not only formed part of the chassis, but was set at an angle so that the prop-shaft passed to the rear-mounted gearbox and final drive assembly down one side of the car, allowing the driver to sit very low beside it. The polar moment of inertia was kept low by locating both engine and transaxle well within the wheelbase, and as a further refinement the petrol was carried in a pair of side tanks on either side of the body so that changes in fuel load had no influence on weight distribution.

Despite this advanced thinking, the car had tremendous handling problems at first and was withdrawn from early entries for further development, not making its first appearance until the Barcelona Grand Prix of October 1954. But Villoresi spun one of the team cars, and although Ascari led for several laps in the other, he was eventually forced to retire, putting Lancia out of the running. The Argentinian Grand Prix of the following year, held at Buenos Aires, was attacked with great expense, but again with no result, both cars spinning off.

But with the Italian Grand Prix later in 1955, everything started to come right for the Lancia team which took first, third and fourth places against the might of Mercedes who had Moss and Fangio driving for them. This success was followed with second places in the Pau and Monaco Grands Prix. Shortly after this however, one of the team's most senior drivers, Alberto Ascari lost his life while testing a car – in fact a Ferrari sports-racer – in an accident which was never fully explained.

Devastated by this catastrophe and under ever increasing financial pressure, the Lancia team decided to withdraw. But instead of scrapping the cars, it was decided in July 1955 to hand them over to Ferrari to exploit their full potential and 'With the intention of promoting the technical advancement of racing cars, which are part of the glorious tradition of the Italian motor industry and add prestige to Italian products throughout the world . . .' In this way Lancia and Ferrari were brought together on the Grand Prix circuits.

Despite many unsympathetic modifications, Ferrari took the D50 to a string of wins in the next few years, helped by the retirement of Mercedes from racing and the enlistment of Fangio as a principal driver.

November the Stratos swiftly accumulated a major string of victories, winning the San Remo, Giro d'Italia, Rideau Lakes and Tour de Corse rallies, placing second in the RAC Rally. The Giro d'Italia win was achieved by Andruet and 'Biche' in a turbocharged car. In combination with supporting wins in the Fulvia HF 1600 and the Beta coupe, these successes gave Lancia the 1974 World Rally Championship with a comfortable 94 points compared to the 69 gained by the runner-up, Fiat.

In 1975 Alitalia replaced Marlboro as the major sponsors, the Stratos began to sprout wings and spoilers and it proceeded to confirm its crushing superiority over all opposition with nine wins, two second places, one third place and two fourth places in major international rallies. The Scandinavian drivers Waldegaard and Thorszelius contributed to this record of success, as did the French drivers Darniche and Mahe driving a car sponsored by Chardonnet, the Lancia importers in France. Once again Lancia became comfortable winners of the World Rally Championship.

One of the most epic struggles of the season took place on the notoriously demanding Safari rally. The three cars entered were extensively modified to cope with the special conditions. The suspension travel was increased from 4in (10cm) to 7in (18cm), a special dust filter system was fitted to the engine air intake, a cradle was built to carry a second spare wheel on the roof and protective cages were added at front and rear. But despite elaborate preparations, an outright win eluded the team. The Munari/Drews car came second after suffering no fewer than eleven flat tyres, the Waldegaard/Thorszelius car managed third place despite three hours lost through gearbox trouble, and the Preston/Ulyate car finished eleventh.

A similar pattern of success was achieved the following year, 1976, even though the Stratos was little changed and Fiat had cut back spending on the Lancia rally programme. It didn't stop the Stratos from accumulating numerous wins in major international rallies which gave them the World Rally Championship with 112 points to Opel's 54. Although Munari scored four of those wins, it was a particularly good year for Darniche and Mahe who also won the European Rally Drivers' Championship. The British Chequered Flag team, who had many problems with their privately entered car, also achieved a win this year – in the Mintex Rally driven by Andy Dawson.

The Stratos team additionally entered cars for circuit racing in 1976, using a second-generation turbocharged power unit masterminded by Mike Parkes with the help of Carlo Facetti and considerably more sophisticated than the earlier turbocharged engine. Retaining the four-valve combustion chambers of the works rally car, it had Kugelfischer fuel injection and a KKK turbocharger with an intercooler and wastegate. The power output was around 500bhp, but the car was not very successful, catching fire at Mugello and forcing the drivers, Facetti and Brambilla, to retire. A car driven by two ladies, however, Lella Lombardi and Christine Dacrement, finished 20th at Le Mans.

DECLINE

After winning three World Rally Championships in a row, the Stratos might well have gone on to win a fourth, but for a change of policy. For marketing reasons Fiat decided at the beginning of 1977 to concentrate their rally efforts on their 131 model, restricting the Stratos to a limited number of events. As a result Fiat won the World Rally Championship that year, but the Stratos also managed to win several major events including the Monte Carlo, Firestone and Total rallies. At the end of the season, though, came another blow to the car's fortunes: the regulations changed, forbidding the four-valve cylinderheads that had helped the works' car to win.

Even so, privately entered cars went on accumulating wins for several more years, until further changes in the rallying regulations made the car ineligible for major rallies.

RENAISSANCE

For some years after its departure from the rally scene, the Stratos sank into obscurity. It no longer had a role in competition and was considered a rather pointless and impractical car for the road. But many a young rally enthusiast retained nostalgic memories of that small shape, a blur of colour, howling through a special section. Gradually, from the early eighties onwards, dedicated enthusiasts of this sort began to acquire examples of the car.

With three provisos, the Stratos was soon discovered to be immense fun to drive on the road. The first proviso is that there is insufficient space inside it for a driver more than about 5ft 10in (1.77m) tall. The second is, as already mentioned, that the car will quickly oversteer if the throttle is eased in a bend, so a certain skill and caution is needed when driving on twisty roads. And the third follows from the marked lack of threequarter rear visibility in a Stratos; at angled T-junctions it has to be driven like a van and placed at right angles to the road being entered. In addition, of course, there is another disadvantage for UK owners, since the car was only ever made in left-hand drive form.

But there are a number of compensations for these limitations. One of the biggest, perhaps, is the marvellous compactness of the car which combines with its supportive seats and snug interior layout to make the driver and passenger feel completely at one with it. Rather pretentiously, perhaps, Nuccio Bertone had originally claimed that the body of the Stratos 'hugged the driver and co-driver like an athlete's tracksuit, so much so that you could almost see their muscles.' But the view was later endorsed by Emerson Fittipaldi who said 'the driver can feel the car almost as if it were sewn on.' From a racing driver, inclined to take such a factor for granted in single seaters, this is quite a tribute.

Excellent performance is another compensation. As the Stratos is lighter than a 246 Dino, and lower-geared, its acceleration is better. Authoritative road-test figures are hard to come by, but the evidence suggests that a good Stratos should beat the Dinos 0–60mph (0–96.5kph) acceleration time of 7.1sec (*Motor*) by half a second or more, and the 0–100mph (0–161kph) acceleration time (*Motor*) of 17.6sec by up to two seconds. The Stratos has a lower top speed, however, of around 140mph.

It also has a very hard and bumpy ride, but it is surprisingly quiet and its rear boot is big enough for a reasonable quota of weekend luggage. Even more than for the Dino, however, this luggage compartment is nicely cooked by the nearby exhaust system, so it is inadvisable to use it for the stowage of such perishables as butter or eggs – the result at the end of the journey could be an accidental and rather messy omelette!

Unfortunately, increased appreciation of the virtues of the Stratos has led to a major rise in its value. Whereas an example could be bought in Germany for £6–7,000 in around 1980, the price quickly rose to £12–20,000 two years later and was up to about £30,000 in 1986, while at the time of writing (summer 1989) the going price was £70–100,000.

8 Ownership

If you do not already own a Dino, be warned: it is expensive to buy, expensive to restore and difficult to service. Unless it has been comprehensively rebuilt or meticulously maintained, it may well be in poor condition, for it was not a durable car when it left the factory. Italian specialist coachbuilders have never been noted for the thoroughness of their anti-corrosion measures or for the quality of their wiring. And although the engine is immensely robust in many respects, it has its weaknesses including a vulnerability to rapid camshaft wear. Moreover, while nearly all Dinos were probably well looked after for the first few years of their life, a large number were later subjected to long periods of neglect during the Energy Crisis of the mid-seventies when their secondhand value fell to its lowest ebb relative to the cost of living. Many cars were then owned by people who either couldn't afford or couldn't be bothered to maintain and repair them properly.

These factors are now dominated by the extent to which the value of the Dino — in common with all other Ferraris — has soared recently. In 1986 it was possible to pick up an example in Britain for around £15,000. But in the following year the average price doubled to around £30,000, doubled again in 1988, the year after that, and has continued to rise since. At the time of writing (summer 1989) dealers were asking £100,000–£110,000 for a good GT model and £120,000–£135,000 for a good GTS, with similar prices being obtained at auction, although privately-sold examples may have exchanged hands for a little less. In May 1989, however, one immaculate low-mileage GT Dino was being offered by a dealer for £150,000.

It seems that the stock market crash of October 1987 may have caused the wealthy to seek alternative forms of investment and thus have been partly responsible for this rapid rise in prices. Certainly the market for Dinos is now influenced, to some extent at least, by 'investors' who never drive the cars themselves but see them merely as objects of profit. To the discerning enthusiast, wishing to enjoy an outstanding classic, this is clearly not a welcome trend.

Barring some major financial or political catastrophe, however, it is not likely to be reversed, so prices will very probably have risen still further by the time this book appears in print. One reason is that the new price levels are partly self-sustaining because they are influenced by labour costs — which seem likely to increase year by year for the foreseeable future. Thus a businessman can now buy a complete wreck for, say, £50,000 and spend £40,000 on its total ground-up restoration (summer 1989 prices again). Only total desperation combined with a slump in the market would then force him to part with the car for less than his total investment of £90,000, and it is far more likely that the end result will be worth considerably more than the original stake. As labour costs increase, so will the cost of restoration, raising the general value of the Dino at least in line with inflation.

Unfortunately this background has engendered an 'if you have to ask the price you can't afford it' attitude amongst certain specialist repairers and restorers. For the less scrupulous of these, it has also presented opportunities for fraudulent combinations of shoddy workmanship and outrageous charges.

These general considerations apply largely

Many cars have suffered extensive neglect, but recent rises in value have made even the worst of them worth restoration.

to the 246 Dino: the 206 is something of a special case. Its aluminium bodywork should be less prone to corrosion than that of the 246, and its extreme rarity makes it even more valuable. It is difficult to put a price on this model, however, since examples change hands relatively infrequently.

ACQUISITION

In many cases the buyer of a Dino will be fulfilling a lifelong ambition and will complete his or her purchase completely blinded by feelings of exhilaration to any faults in their new acquisition. But if you can force yourself to take a cooler and more cautious attitude, it pays.

There are two golden rules, the first of which is *to speak to as many existing Dino owners as possible*. If you already own a Ferrari of another sort, this is easy: you join the Ferrari Owners' Club (see useful addresses page 180). If you do not, you will be eligible to join its affiliated group for non-owning enthusiasts, the Prancing Horse Register. In both cases you will be able to attend the numerous test days laid on by the club, and to purchase a copy of an extremely valuable book, the *Ferrari Register*. This is an amazing work of reference which contains the names and addresses of all past and present Ferrari Owners' Club members with details of the cars owned by them currently and in the past, all extensively cross-indexed against such factors as area, model, chassis number and registration number. It also contains a good deal of extremely useful historical information on both racing and road-going Ferraris of all types.

With the help of this book and attendance at test days you should have no problem contacting existing Dino owners and you will generally find them happy to talk freely about the problems of ownership with a fellow enthusiast. From them you will be able to learn roughly how much repairs or rebuilds cost, and, most important of all, *which repairers and restorers are currently believed to be honest and reliable*. This leads immediately to the second golden rule which is that you should *never assume that advertisements placed in club literature or elsewhere are any guarantee of the integrity of those placing them*. Most of the dealers and repairs who so advertise, are indeed reputable companies, but some are not. Finding out which is which brings us back to golden rule number one: *to speak to as many existing Dino owners as possible*.

There are several good reasons why caution is needed here. The first is that the combination of remote investors lacking personal interest in their cars with the large amounts of money now changing hands for repair and restoration work together present splendid opportunities for the dishonest. As a result, a number of owners have in recent years been grossly overcharged for work that was shoddy, and in some cases, not done at all. A second reason is that the highly skilled panel beaters and mechanics crucial to the proper functioning of a particular small firm sometimes leave, causing the standard of workmanship to drop sharply. A third is that the general efficiency of these small companies often waxes and wanes: their managements change or become careless and greedy over the years, and the value for money they offer rises or falls accordingly. There is thus no substitute for up-to-date personal recommendation.

Having identified one or more small firms known to be currently honest and reliable, the next step is to make friends with the principal of one of them. When you have found a car you want to buy, ask him to come along and give an opinion on its condition. The £50–100 you may have to pay for his time will probably be more valuable than a similar sum spent on an AA or RAC survey, admirable though those may be. For specialised knowledge is needed to spot the subtle thickening of the body lines where

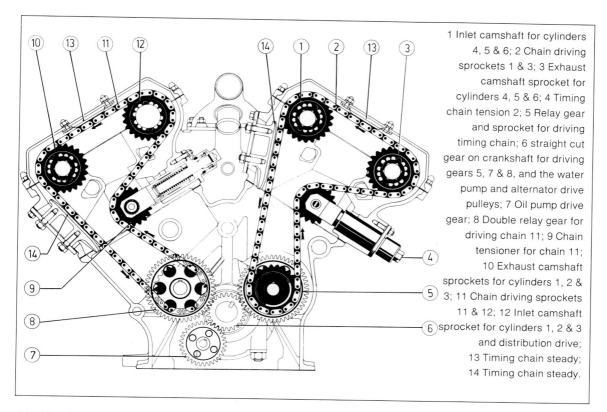

1 Inlet camshaft for cylinders 4, 5 & 6; 2 Chain driving sprockets 1 & 3; 3 Exhaust camshaft sprocket for cylinders 4, 5 & 6; 4 Timing chain tension 2; 5 Relay gear and sprocket for driving timing chain; 6 straight cut gear on crankshaft for driving gears 5, 7 & 8, and the water pump and alternator drive pulleys; 7 Oil pump drive gear; 8 Double relay gear for driving chain 11; 9 Chain tensioner for chain 11; 10 Exhaust camshaft sprockets for cylinders 1, 2 & 3; 11 Chain driving sprockets 11 & 12; 12 Inlet camshaft sprocket for cylinders 1, 2 & 3 and distribution drive; 13 Timing chain steady; 14 Timing chain steady.

246 Camshaft drive – note tensioners.

filler is covering rust or to detect other similar tell-tale indications of poor condition peculiar to the car. The final decision, of course, can only be yours – the *caveat emptor* principle, let the buyer beware, overrides all others here – but disinterested expert advice is generally helpful.

The Dinos for sale that you examine may roughly speaking be expected to fall into one of four categories: the completely and properly rebuilt, the original but well maintained, the bodged, and the unrestored in poor condition. For cars in the first category, the properly rebuilt, the price will be high and your task, apart from assessing the direct physical evidence, will be to check that it has indeed been properly rebuilt and by a reputable company doing good work at the time. If satisfactory answers to these questions are obtained, you should have a car which will be a joy to own for many years.

Cars in good original condition and said to be well maintained need to be viewed with considerable suspicion. Almost certainly they will have needed some bodywork repair during their lives such as new sills and door bottoms, while unless meticulously maintained, engines tend to need major attention, at 30–40,000 miles. If the necessary repairs have been done well, then no problems should arise, but if not, expensive further work may be needed. If you are unable to contact all the previous owners and obtain satisfactory answers from them, you would be advised to pass on and look elsewhere.

Mileage claims, too, need careful attention. It is very difficult to believe the 10–15,000 miles sometimes claimed for 'low-mileage-cars, all of which must be a minimum of fifteen years of age by the summer of 1989, the time of writing. There cannot, surely be

Rusting sills: a common affliction.

many owners or succession of owners who drove their Dinos as little as 700–800 miles a year for many years. A two-mile trip from home to the station and back every working day for a year would alone involve a total of at least 1,000 miles, excluding any shopping or holiday mileage. Even when bought as a second, 'fun' car, a pleasure mileage of 2–3,000 a year is much more likely, making a minimum total mileage of 30–45,000 more plausible for a genuine low mileage car. It's just possible that a car might have been stored in a garage or the proverbial dry barn for some years, but the claim should be disbelieved if it cannot be independently verified. In fact, of course, the vast majority of cars will have covered a minimum of 60–180,000 miles – whatever the odometer may say – during their lives of 15–20 years.

More difficult still will be the assessment of cars said to have been rebuilt or properly maintained but which have in fact been extensively bodged. Quite a lot of the work now being undertaken by the reputable restoration companies involves undoing or correcting the mistakes perpetrated by previous cowboy repairers. Simply identifying such a car may not be at all easy, and in such cases the experience and expert knowledge of a reputable repairer will prove invaluable. Obviously the car's history will be equally important – an investigation into it may quickly reveal that it has been subjected to short-term cosmetic repairs by companies with a bad reputation.

In many ways a car honestly admitted to be unrestored and in mediocre or poor condition may be the best buy – so long as you pay the appropriately low price for it and have another £40,000 or so in hand to pay for a ground-up rebuild. But expert knowledge is again important, since such cars can be beyond restoration at a reasonable price. Spare engines are very hard to find, for

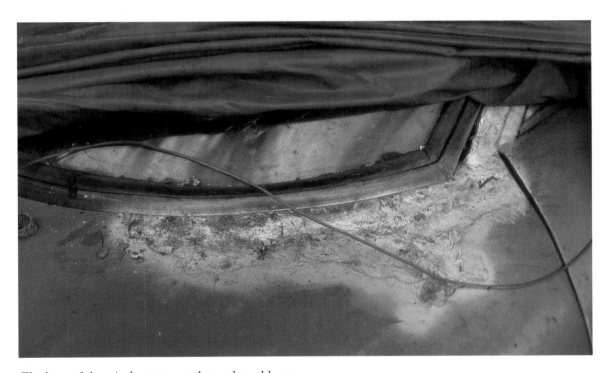

The base of the windscreen: another vulnerable area.

instance, so a power unit with a badly damaged cylinder block could add several thousand pounds to the bill.

WEAKNESSES

Chassis and body

In its original 206 form the Dino was built around a relatively simple chassis of oval-section and square-section tubes with a central ladder-like frame joining raised structures which support the front suspension at one end of the car and the engine and rear suspension at the other. This chassis provides the majority of the structural strength and torsional stiffness. Except perhaps for the roof structure which bridges the central cockpit area, the aluminum bodywork contributed little to the overall torsional rigidity.

For the 246 model the chassis retained its basic design but was considerably strengthened, larger section tubes being used in many areas. Again, it was the chassis rather than the body — now made of steel — which provided the bulk of the strength and stiffness. The steel roof, however, clearly does make a useful contribution to the overall stiffness, since a GT model is noticeably more rigid than a GTS model with its open top. A 246GT in good condition does not suffer at all from 'scuttle shake' — high-frequency transverse movements of the structure around the dashboard — on bumpy surfaces. On bumpy surfaces it is also totally vice free in its handling, proof that the suspension geometry is not being disturbed by flexing of the chassis or 'fifth spring' as it is sometimes called. The GTS model, on the other hand, tends to creak and rattle on bumpy roads, despite strengthening in the framework bay just ahead of the engine.

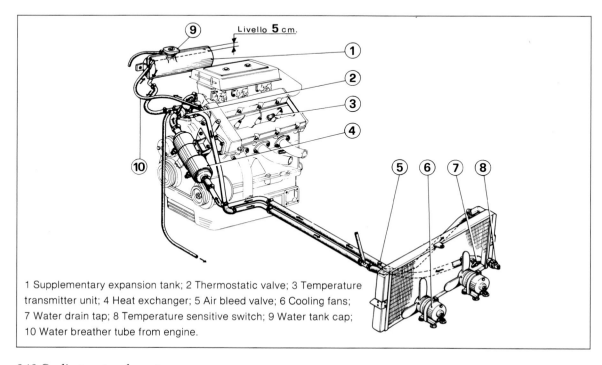

1 Supplementary expansion tank; 2 Thermostatic valve; 3 Temperature transmitter unit; 4 Heat exchanger; 5 Air bleed valve; 6 Cooling fans; 7 Water drain tap; 8 Temperature sensitive switch; 9 Water tank cap; 10 Water breather tube from engine.

246 Cooling system layout.

Using a design approach which was very advanced for the time, this body/chassis was finished off with a number of glass fibre panels attached to it with rivets or bolts. All four wheelarch liners are made of glass fibre, as are an undertray riveted to the bottom of the chassis and a floor for the cockpit fixed to the top of it. The good news is that these glass fibre panels successfully protected the chassis and inner parts of the body against abrasion; the bad news is that they also created water traps and that neither the body nor the chassis were well protected against rust.

The net result is that all cars that have not been rebuilt or carefully repaired are likely to be heavily corroded, particularly below the waistline, whatever the external paintwork may temporarily say to the contrary – our photographs illustrate some of the early and not-so-early warning signs to look out for, as well as the extent of exposed rust in bad cases. The door bottoms and sills are usually the first to go, these being followed by the wheelarches and the vulnerable front nose-cone structure. Rust is often discovered higher up, too, around the headlamps, the tops of the doors and the base of the windscreen where the rubber strip that seals the glass often fails, creating leaks into the footwells and causing local corrosion of the metal just beneath it.

Generally the chassis is not as badly affected, but thanks to the entrapment of water by the glass fibre undertray, there can sometimes be severe corrosion at the junctions between the side-members and the cross-members. For this reason, removal of the riveted undertray, if (unlikely) the owner will allow it, greatly facilitates an assessment of a car's overall condition when buying. Occasionally the central oval tube is also corroded.

A full catalogue of these horrors makes for depressing reading, but everything can be repaired and made as new (see page 186 for details).

Engine

Both the 2-litre light alloy engine of the 206 and the 2.4-litre cast iron engine of the 246 are immensely strong and in racing form developed power outputs far greater than in standard road-going tune. The four-valve Stratos versions of the unit, for instance, eventually developed around 270bhp in naturally aspirated form and close to 500bhp with a turbocharger.

Despite this inherent strength, the 246 engine on which we concentrate here has its oddities and weaknesses. Its oil pressure, for example, is not the reliable sympton of basic engine health that it usually is, because the electric oil pressure gauge is notoriously inaccurate and unreliable. Its sensor, too, is often a cause of oil leaks. An experienced Dino repairer will possess an accurate mechanical gauge which can be substituted for the electric sensor to obtain a reliable reading.

The engine's basic weakness is premature camshaft wear, though there is controversy about both the cause and extent of this. Some repairers say that it was largely confined to an early batch of engines fitted with inadequately hardened tappet shims – wear of the shims increases the clearance and soon leads to wear of the camshaft itself. Others say that all engines are affected and that the basic cause is an inherently insufficient flow of oil to the camshafts at low engine speeds. An engine that spends a lot of time in traffic will suffer rapid camshaft wear, it is said, while one that is consistently thrashed at high rpm on country lanes or circuits will not.

Most agree, though, that the problem does exist but believe that it is much alleviated by careful servicing in which the tappet clearances are checked and adjusted if necessary at 3,000–mile intervals instead of the prescribed 6,000–mile intervals.

Another, but lesser, valvegear problem may be found in early engines fitted with timing chain tensioners which could move

A door 'inner' (above) − also prone to
rust but seen here repaired.

New pieces have been patched in here
(below) but complete front ends are still available
from the factory.

out of engagement; a locking bolt modification was introduced to cure the problem and very few units now lack this.

The ignition system is a further source of trouble, though often it is easily curable. The distributor is grossly inaccessible and may need rebuilding from time to time, but it is not the only cause of difficulty. Dinos were originally fitted with the Marelli Dinoplex system, an early form of transistor-assisted capacitative discharge electronic ignition in which Ferrari clearly had little confidence, since all cars were also fitted with an additional conventional system with its own separate coil which could be brought into action in an emergency. Few of the original Dinoplex systems are still operational, but it would be unwise to rely wholly on the conventional alternative: a six-cylinder engine turning over at up to 7,800rpm requires a lot of sparks every minute. A modern electronic system is a good investment, but in place of the very expensive (£568.49 including VAT; summer 1989) Ferrari replacement for the Dinoplex system, a much less expensive proprietary kit such as the Sparkrite SX 2000 will do just as well.

The cooling of the engine – always critical when it is mounted in the middle of the car – is yet another area of concern. The radiator may well need rebuilding, or at least to be carefully flushed clean, and attention should be paid to the two (rather undersized) electric cooling fans and their thermostat whose proper functioning is essential to thermal equilibrium in a summer traffic jam. The radiator is fed through a pair of flexible armoured hoses running from one end of the car to the other which may leak or clog up, impairing cooling efficiency.

Additional cooling is provided by a small oil/water heat exchanger, mounted just above the engine. This, too, can become obstructed – with the result that oil temperature may continue to rise when the water temperature is stable. It is not easy to

Glassfibre liners originally protected wheel-arches but didn't block ingress of water.

Bodywork repairs involve highly skilled panel beating.

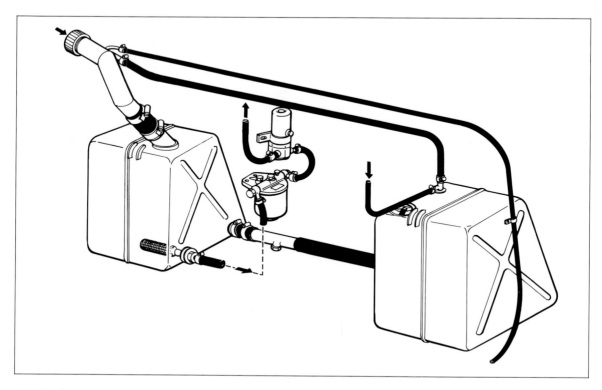

246 Fuel system.

clean out, so owners contemplating a rebuild might be advised to consider the possibility of having a separate front-mounted oil cooler fitted.

Despite being fitted with a flow-and-return fuel system, the Dino is inherently liable to vapour lock and is thus always difficult to start from hot in warm weather – it may even misfire for 2–3 minutes before a proper flow of fuel is re-established. While this is a quirk of the car that has to be tolerated, the leaks which the fuel system sometimes suffers are clearly less acceptable. These mainly occur because the two aluminium fuel tanks are protected with a bitumastic compound which tends to lose adhesion, trapping moisture and causing corrosion, especially underneath where the tanks rest on pads of a fabric material which also absorbs moisture. Thus areas of the tanks may develop leaks;

sometimes the aluminium merely becomes porous – a faint but persistent smell of petrol is often an indication of this fault. New pieces of aluminium can be welded into an affected tank and an alternative material – say rubber – substituted for the pad beneath.

Transmission

Another quirk of the car which has to be accepted, and which is common to other Ferrari models, is the difficulty of engaging second gear until the gearbox oil has been warmed up by a mile or two of running. Adjustment of the control rod and cable is critical, and sometimes the inherently weak second gear synchromesh can wear so much that the ratio is difficult to select even when the gearbox oil is hot. A transmission overhaul will then be necessary, but this fault apart the gearbox is generally robust and long lasting. Adherence to the 6,000 mile oil change interval is important. The clutch, moreover, can be replaced without removing the engine or transmission from the car. If the gearbox has to be rebuilt, replacement of the limited-slip differential should perhaps be considered: its friction clutches are sure to be worn.

Suspension and running gear

Despite having a ground clearance of only 5.5in (13.9cm) a Dino in good condition does not normally bottom, even on the most severe of bumps, though it may ground on steep ramps. Unfortunately, however, the springs tend to sag. If this is not immediately obvious when the car is first viewed, it will soon become so when it is driven. The bottom of the car will foul the slightest incline – watch out for the nose cone which is particularly vulnerable to damage by kerbs. Happily, new springs are readily available, not particularly expensive and the problem is easily cured. The dampers – limited-life components in any case – may similarly need replacement, but these again are readily available and not unreasonable in price for a car of this sort (approximately £75 each including VAT; summer 1989).

The Dino's wishbones are robust and seldom give trouble, but as for all cars built since the early sixties these pivot on insulating bushes which may need replacement from time to time. Straightforward bushes are used at the front, but the rear wishbones pivot on PTFE sleeves which may need attention. If the car darts to the left under power and to the right on the overrun – or vice versa – this is a sure sign of unwanted rear-wheel steering which will probably be cured by bush replacement.

As for all modern cars, the Dino has ball-joints in its steering system which wear after high mileages. There are four in all, at the ends of the two track-rods which link the steering rack to the front wheels, but again these are neither expensive nor difficult to replace. Play in the steering may also be due to slack in the splined sleeve which the steering column incorporates; simply tightening the pinch bolt often cures the problem. If the steering still feels vague, new rubber mounting bushes for the steering rack may be required. These not only affect steering feel but have a crucial influence on the handling of the car as a whole and so should be replaced if their condition is in any way suspect. The steering rack itself, though slender in construction, seldom gives trouble and can be adjusted to take up wear between the pinion and the rack.

At some time in its life almost every Dino will have been subjected to hard driving on twisty roads involving heavy usage of the brakes. Cracked discs, therefore, especially at the front, are a distinct possibility. Replacement discs are available but not cheap (£316 for a front disc and £134 for a rear disc including VAT; summer 1989). The brake pipes can corrode, too, in hidden places such as underneath the engine.

Restoration and repair

Happily for the Dino owner or prospective owner, a wide range of engine, transmission, suspension and body parts are available. These 'Marpart' components, either original or remanufactured to the original specifications, are available from the UK Ferrari importers, Maranello Concessionaires Ltd, based in Egham, Surrey (see useful addresses – page 182). Some of these parts are quite reasonably priced – a set of front brake pads for £23.83, for instance, while drivers' handbooks and workshop manuals are also available at sensible prices. Similarly, £184 is not expensive for a new door skin, and £253 quite modest for the unusual and highly-curved rear screen. And a complete new bodywork front-end back to the front bulkhead – wings, bonnet-lid surround, etc − can be obtained (after a long wait) for around £3,000 − pretty fair for a low-volume prestige car that has been out of production since 1974.

But some other parts are very much more expensive, such as camshafts at around £300, cylinder heads for about £1,400 and fuel tanks which cost about £300 (right hand) or about £340 (left hand). Marpart starter motors were unavailable at the time of writing, but alternatives from an Italian source said to be available at £1,600. (All prices include VAT and are as at summer 1989.)

While a major repair for a Dino or a complete restoration of one is never going to be cheap, the availability of these parts not only facilitates work but also makes it much easier for an owner to retain careful control over expenditure. Parts prices can quickly be obtained by telephoning the Marpart depot (see page 182 for number) and are also published in regular parts information bulletins distributed free to members of the Ferrari Owners' Club.

With this information at hand, and knowing the hourly rate of the workshop involved, controlling the cost of a repair should be no more difficult than for a modern car. An extensive restoration or complete rebuild, however, calls for a good deal more care − costs can all too easily get out of hand and large sums of money are involved. At the time of writing the going price for an extensive restoration seemed to be around £25,000, and while some companies were quoting £30−35,000 for a complete rebuild, others were quoting £40−45,000.

Door skins are available and relatively inexpensive.

Camshafts are prone to premature wear unless maintenance is meticulous.

A form of psychological trap is often involved, too. Many Dino owners who pursue cost-cutting exercises in their business or professional lives with ruthless shrewdness, develop an emotional soft spot for their car. They treat it as indulgently as a spoilt child and tell themselves that nothing is too good for it and so they must expect to pay high prices for good work. Unfortunately, if they do not exercise the same caution that they apply to business matters, they may all too easily end up paying high prices for bad work – bad work that often has to be done again. For this reason we include the advice that follows, though most of it is pretty obvious.

When planning a major renovation project, therefore, the first step is to define very carefully exactly what you want. If your car is in fair rather than poor condition, it could be that piecing in new areas of metal below the waistline may suffice for the bodywork, leaving the car with its original wiring harness and cockpit trim. Some Dinos are being grossly over-trimmed these days, giving their interiors a look of over-stuffed luxury quite uncharacteristic of the original cars. And since the wiring has the normal long-lasting plastic insulation that has been in use for decades, trimming the leads to expose and solder new bare ends may be all that's necessary to ensure future reliability. Alternatively, you might wish everything to be removed and body and chassis to be stripped back to bare metal. And when it comes to the external paint finish, you may want it to be of concours perfection rather than merely a job well done.

Having made these decisions, the next stage, as in all business matters of this sort, is to approach a number – say three – of repairers for detailed quotations. If your car is not a runner, you'll probably find that the principals of the firms approached will be prepared to conduct no-charge inspections of

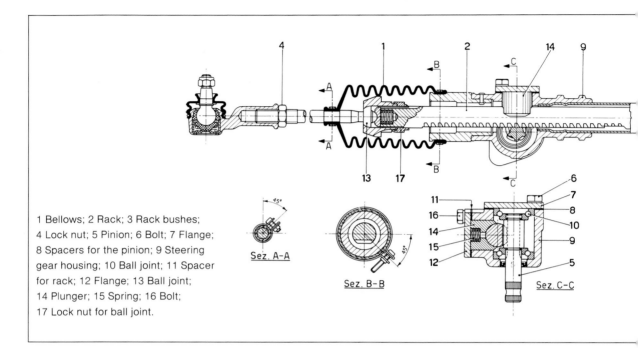

1 Bellows; 2 Rack; 3 Rack bushes;
4 Lock nut; 5 Pinion; 6 Bolt; 7 Flange;
8 Spacers for the pinion; 9 Steering
gear housing; 10 Ball joint; 11 Spacer
for rack; 12 Flange; 13 Ball joint;
14 Plunger; 15 Spring; 16 Bolt;
17 Lock nut for ball joint.

Sez. A–A

Sez. B–B

Sez. C–C

246 Rack and pinion steering gear.

it at your premises. Quite understandably, few restorers will agree to a fixed and binding price for fear of the unforeseen problems that may arise. Corroded cylinder heads may be all but impossible to lift, and the removal of a trim panel may uncover a large area of hitherto unsuspected rust.

Nevertheless you should subject their estimates to careful scrutiny and insist that labour and parts costs be separated. You can then subject them to a little commonsense cross-checking of your own. As a very rough guide, for instance, labour costs for mechanical work should be about half parts costs, whereas labour costs for bodywork repairs are likely to cost more than double material and parts costs. At the time of writing for instance, a typical engine rebuild calls for around £5,000 worth of new parts but should not involve much more than three man-weeks of work: a week for disassembly, a week for cleaning, machining and fitting

and a week for reassembly. Even at the high rate of £25 an hour, this involves a labour charge of no more than £3,000.

For a substantial bodywork project, though, the cost emphasis is likely to be reversed. Even if a complete front end is required at £3,000, the total cost of this and other body parts such as door skins plus quantities of lead, paint, sheet steel and aluminium should not exceed £5,000. But proper bodywork repairs are very labour intensive and require high levels of skill, so the associated labour cost is likely to be at least £10,000. Be wary, though. To take an arbitrary example, a labour cost of £15,000 means fifteen 40–hour weeks at £25 an hour, and one properly-supervised skilled man can do a very great deal of work in nearly four months. Without careful control, you may find yourself being asked for large sums of money that have not been properly accounted for.

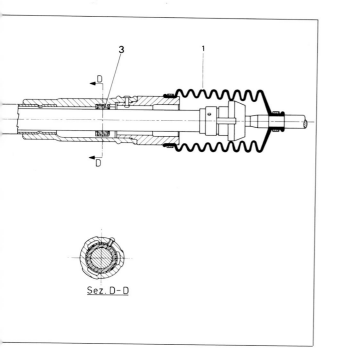

Sez. D-D

Once an estimate has been agreed, the next step is to ensure that its precise terms are confirmed by you in writing. You should then follow this up by inspecting the work done at regular intervals. It is particularly important to make such an inspection when engine/transmission disassembly is complete, as you can then discuss with the repairer the extent to which new parts are needed. Similarly, it's crucial to pay a visit when the bodywork has been exposed to the agreed extent so that all the damaged or corroded areas are clearly visible. But even when rebuilding work is well in hand, it's important to inspect progress at intervals no longer than three weeks – at the least this will discourage the repairer from discontinuing work on your car to complete some rush job.

At each of these visits you should summarise, again in writing, the progress made, with any relevant comments. It is vital that any extra charges required by the repairer due to unforeseen problems be

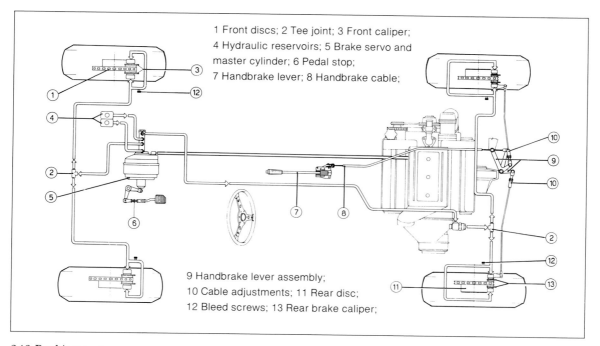

1 Front discs; 2 Tee joint; 3 Front caliper;
4 Hydraulic reservoirs; 5 Brake servo and
master cylinder; 6 Pedal stop;
7 Handbrake lever; 8 Handbrake cable;

9 Handbrake lever assembly;
10 Cable adjustments; 11 Rear disc;
12 Bleed screws; 13 Rear brake caliper;

246 Braking system.

Moisture can penetrate under the bituminous coating (here removed) of the two light alloy fuel tanks causing corrosion. Porous areas are not uncommon.

carefully agreed in writing at each of these stages, as should any extras required by yourself. All this may irritate the repairer — paperwork is not usually the strong point of the small companies generally involved — but nevertheless a proper record of the project in writing is fair to everyone in the long run.

Upper seat belt attachment is anchored to the rear window surround — it is worth checking for structural integrity and reinforcing if necessary.

SERVICING

The Dino is not an easy car to service and maintain. The problems start with its low ground clearance and tightly enclosed engine/transmission unit which combine to make accessibility distinctly poor. Even so simple a task as topping up the engine oil is difficult: the oil filler cap of the forward cylinder bank is awkwardly tucked away under the hinged engine cover while the filler cap of the rear cylinder bank is rendered unusable by a hose routed over the top of it. Similarly the plugs in the forward bank of cylinders can only be undone with an extension bar and universal joint in the socket drive, and to get at the distributor it's necessary to remove the rear offside wheel and unbolt its detachable wheelarch liner.

To compound these difficulties, the schedule of routine servicing tasks is lengthy and the 3,000-mile intervals specified would now be regarded as quite unacceptably short — though probably of little inconvenience to current owners. Many of the tasks listed for attention at these intervals are merely checks, but some, such as lubrication of the distributor cam and (on earlier cars) of the front ball joints, are not. Modern components and materials, though, have perhaps made a few of the requirements less urgent today than when the car was first built. Both the brake fluid and the sparking plugs, for example, might reasonably be expected to last a good deal longer than the 6,000 miles originally set as the limit.

But owners might be advised to stick to the original 6,000-mile intervals for engine oil changes — or even to change oil at 3,000 mile intervals — worth it to preserve a precious asset. Similarly, they are advised to have the valve clearances checked every 3,000 miles and adjusted if necessary.

Generally speaking major engine or transmission repairs or rebuilds are jobs for skilled and experienced mechanics with the proper Ferrari training.

9 Activities

Today there are more opportunities in Britain than ever before to learn about your Dino and to enjoy it in the company of like-minded fellow owners. If you're seeking technical expertise or just want to gossip, if you need moral support in a rebuild crisis or you plan to take up racing, you'll find no lack of knowledgeable and sympathetic people to talk to.

THE FERRARI OWNERS' CLUB

The key to all these contacts is your national Ferrari club: there's one in every major European country as well as in many more distant countries such as the USA, Japan and Australia. What's more there are clubs specifically for Dino owners in Switzerland

People dream of owning one Ferrari Dino in their lifetime — but to own two . . . !

and Japan. In Britain the Ferrari Owners' Club (FOC) has some 1,400 members and is one of the most prosperous and thriving one-make organisations in the country. All past and present Ferrari owners are eligible to join, and while the annual subscription may seem steep at £50 (valid for 1990) most regard the money as well spent. This £50 automatically buys membership for wives or husbands as well as yourself, and the club organises a wide range of activities, all of which have a strong social element. It keeps members informed through an attractively produced bi-monthly newsletter which comes free with the subscription and in addition publishes *Ferrari*, a glossy quarterly which is available for an additional charge (£10 annually in the UK at the time of writing). The Ferrari Owners' Club also maintains links with Ferrari Clubs abroad – there are more than 20 of them.

If you are a prospective rather than an actual owner, you may, as already mentioned, join an affiliated group, the Prancing Horse Register for non-owning enthusiasts (subscription £15). Membership will entitle you to attend all Ferrari Owners' Club events, to act as a marshal, time-keeper's assistant or in other ways, but not to compete in races, sprints or hillclimbs.

It is these test days which are perhaps the most enjoyable and useful of the events organised. They present owners with the opportunity to drive their cars as they are meant to be driven – without risk of prosecution for exceeding a speed limit – on a motor racing circuit hired exclusively for the occasion. At the time of writing (summer 1989) the FOC itself was regularly organising one such test day annually – at Castle Combe in early October – but at least three others were being run every year by Modena Engineering Ltd (Castle Combe), Graypaul Motors (Donington Park) and Kent High Performance Cars Ltd (Brands Hatch) – see useful addresses – page 182. Two or three additional test days are often organised

each year by Ferrari dealers or repairers, enthusiastic private individuals or regional branches of the FOC.

If you already have racing or circuit-driving experience, you won't need to be told how enjoyable these events are, and what excellent opportunities they offer to smarten up the neatness and precision of one's high-speed driving. If you've never driven on a circuit before, however, don't be afraid; you'll soon find your way round and begin to enjoy it. Neither previous experience nor a competition licence is needed, and skilled instructors are always in attendance to show you the best lines through the corners, should you ask for help. Hitching a ride as a passenger with someone who is really quick is usually an educational and worthwhile experience, too. The wearing of crash helmets for obvious safety reasons is generally the only requirement (apart from payment of a charge for the day) though in some cases the cars are scrutineered to ensure that they have effective brakes, secure throttle-return springs and so on.

Even if you don't drive your Dino on the track at all, the occasion is usually a very pleasant day out for wives and girlfriends as well as the menfolk with plenty of time to look at some beautiful cars and talk to other owners. An excellent lunch generally forms part of the proceedings, which often include organised or impromptu dinner parties at nearby hotels.

In any given year the Ferrari Owners' Club also organises several weekend get-togethers for their members at hotels which are generally luxurious but usually reasonable in price. Furthermore, FOC members are regularly invited by overseas Ferrari clubs to events abroad, often involving racing or a test day at such circuits as Dijon, Zolder or Zandvoort. In addition to the usual AGM and annual dinner-dance, the FOC also runs an annual *concours d'elegance* – which in recent years has been held at Brocket Hall in Hertfordshire. Even if you consider your own

A left-hand drive 246GTS. Swivelling louvres on the facia were the only means of admitting screen or face-level air with the Targa top in place.

car to be far too rusty, scruffy and fraying at the edges to enter, this is another event well worth attending for the opportunity it offers to look at some superb cars and talk to their owners.

COMPETITION

Acquisition of a Ferrari Dino also offers its owner the opportunity to realise any long-

held secret ambitions to drive competitively. At one end of the scale involvement can be as low-key as occasional participation in hillclimbs or sprints (short events on closed

The Ferrari Owners' Club organises a variety of meetings and weekend get-togethers for its members. This array of red 308s and 328s was photographed at the 1989 concours d'elegance held at Brocket Hall in Hertfordshire (see overleaf).

circuits in which competitors race against the clock rather than each other). At the other end of the scale the dedicated motorsport enthusiast can compete in the full eight-race season of the Pirelli Maranello Ferrari Challenge.

Newcomers to motorsport may hesitate at the thought of subjecting a classic car worth £100–150,000 to the brutalities of competition. But a well-prepared Dino in good condition thrives on hard usage, and major accidents are rare. And although some

The driving position of the 308GT4 avoided the Italian short legs/long arms syndrome and provided plenty of room for all but the exceptionally tall.

of the more serious competitors in the Maranello series of races spend a lot of money on their cars, their driving abilities do not always match the depth of their pockets. There are classes for unmodified cars, and a competent driver in a near-standard Dino should be able to do well.

Even though a large selection of hillclimbs, sprints and races is now available to owners, interest in using road-going Ferraris for competition at club level is fairly new. Until quite recently relatively new Ferraris were seen at hillclimbs and sprints, and it was difficult to organise an adequate grid for the annual Ferrari race at Donington Park. All that was changed by the Maranello Ferrari Challenge set up in 1986 by John Swift, competitions secretary of the Ferrari Owners' Club, and sponsored by Maranello Concessionaires Ltd, the UK Ferrari importers.

The series of eight races was open to all road-going Ferraris with few restrictions to modifications. The field was, however, divided into five classes: Class 1 for V6 cars – the 206GT, 246GT and 246GTS; Class 2 for V8 cars – subdivided into Class 2A for the 308GTB, and 2B for the 308GT4; Class 3 for

A 1973 Dino 246GT on the track. Becoming a member of the
Ferrari Owners' Club allows owners the chance to drive their
cars to their full potential.

V12 cars – eg 250GT, 330GTC, 365GTB4, 400GT, etc; and Class 4 for flat 12 cars and Testarossas. For that first season points were awarded only for overall placings in each race and the outright winner of the series was Tony Worswick in a 308GTB. His success set a pattern which has since been followed: the top few drivers tend to have had previous competition experience – Tony Worswick's was in rallying – and to be competing in a 308GTB or 308GT4. The highest-placed Dino, a 246GT driven by Jeff Simpson, came 11th overall with 45 points to Tony Worswick's 155.

For 1987 Michelin joined Maranello as sponsors of the series and some changes were made to the rules, the class structure being changed, as follows:

Class 01: standard V6 and V12 cars
Class 02: standard V8 and flat 12 cars
Class M1: modified V6 and flat 12 cars
Class M2: modified V8, flat 12 and 288GTO.

The rules were framed to ensure that the standard cars were indeed standard except for safety modifications, with RAC-approved road tyres, and could be driven to and from circuits rather than being transported on trailers. Nevertheless careful preparation soon made some cars quicker than others.

Except for flared wheelarches, no changes to body shape were permitted for the modified classes, neither was it allowed to alter the 'principal mechanical components' of the engine, so that turbos or four-valve heads could not be fitted to cars which did not originally have them. This left plenty of scope for tuning, however. One or two of the 308 engines were soon developing outputs claimed to be in excess of 300bhp compared to the 255bhp of the standard engine.

Yet to allow the overall winner of the series to emerge from any class, the usual 9-6-4-3-2-1 points system was applied to each class, subject to reduction if there were only a few starters in that class. But for this restriction Jeff Simpson would have won the series outright in a 246GT, but since there were few starters in Class 01, he came second with a points total cut to 47, compared to the 54 achieved by Robbie Stirling in a 308GTB. An interesting newcomer was Bob Newton, who with no previous competition experience managed to achieve two class wins in an unmodified 308GTB running on a low budget, showing that there's plenty of room for the novice.

From these early beginnings the Maranello Challenge (Michelin continued as co-sponsors for 1988, but their role was taken over by Pirelli for 1989) has become a firmly established feature of the club racing scene in Britain. Other series of events are also open to Dino owners, notably the Goodrich Essex Challenge, principally for sprints and hillclimbs, organised by the Essex branch of the Ferrari Owners' Club.

MARANELLO CONCESSIONAIRES LTD

The development of the Ferrari marque in Britain and the support now available for it owes a great deal to the efforts of one man: the late Colonel R.J. ('Ronnie') Hoare, CBE, founder of Maranello Concessionaires Ltd, the sole UK Ferrari importer. In his youth Colonel Hoare was a keen amateur racing driver, competing in supercharged MGs at Brooklands in the thirties, and driving Aston Martins in races and hillclimbs after the Second World War. He became a Ferrari enthusiast after buying a 250GT in 1959, and acquired the UK Ferrari concession in 1960. For the first six years of its life it operated from two bays of F. English Ltd in Bournemouth, a Ford dealership also owned by Colonel Hoare.

In those days Ferrari sales in Britain were small – the target for the first year of operation was four cars. Each car sold was

Rear view of the GT MkI; the prancing horse badge was not fitted originally.

built to special order, and after a long waiting period was collected by Maranello Concessionaires staff and driven across Europe to Britain, being run-in on the way.

While Ferrari were already famous for their exploits on the circuits of the world, the road-going cars were something of an unknown quantity in Britain at that time and needed promotion. Unable to afford the high cost of national advertising, Colonel Hoare chose instead to concentrate on two forms of publicity: a stand at the annual Motor Show and a programme of racing. Over a period of some seven years the sports and GT Ferraris entered by the Maranello team succeeded in winning numerous international events including the Tourist Trophy, Rheims 12 Hours, Montlhery

The growth of enthusiasm

It was in 1966 that Tony Rippon, a member of the Bugatti Owners' Club, suggested the formation of an associated club for Ferrari owners. Bugattis being rare and precious even then, fewer and fewer of them were being brought to the events staged by the club, so it was thought that the inclusion of an affiliated marque would restore strength to its activities. Ferraris were considered to be very similar in calibre and character to Bugattis, both makes being the creations of strong and highly individualistic men who pursued motor racing with fanatical determination.

Enzo Ferrari's approval was sought and obtained, and in January 1967 the Ferrari Owners' Club Ltd was formed, 93 of its 100 shares being held by the Bugatti Owners' Club, one of each of the remaining shares being allotted to the seven original officials: Jack Perkins (Chairman), Tony Rippon, Hugh Conway, Ronnie Symondson, Godfrey Eaton (Secretary), Peter Hampton and Bernard Kain, all luminaries of the classic car movement. Colonel Ronnie Hoare CBE, founder of the sole UK Ferrari Importers, Maranello Concessionaires Ltd became President of the new club and later its Patron (a post he held until his death in September 1989.)

In those days, although racing success had already made the Ferrari name world famous, there were very few road-going cars in Britain bearing the Prancing Horse emblem, but support for the club grew rapidly nevertheless. Following a turn-out of more than ninety cars at Prescott Hillclimb in 1967, the club started to publish its own newsletter later the same year. It was produced by Godfrey Eaton, a vital driving force in the development of the club, who was to remain its secretary until his retirement in 1987 – originally he was secretary of both the Bugatti Owners' Club and the Ferrari Owners' Club. In 1970 the Ferrari Owners' Club held its first separate event, a rally at the home of member David Griffiths-Hughes. In the same year, Tony Rippon who had succeeded Jack Perkins as chairman, stepped down in favour of Peter Stubberfield, who held the office for many years until he was made President in 1987, Frank Bott becoming Chairman in his place.

By 1972 the club had expanded sufficiently to put on an international rally. Invitations to overseas clubs were sent out, and their owners joined those of the Ferrari Owners' Club at a series of events which included ascents of Prescott, racing at Oulton Park and a visit to Trentham Hall, near Stoke-on-Trent.

Four years later, in 1976, the club broke away from the Bugatti Owners' Club, becoming a separate entity in its own right. It has continued to expand and develop ever since, and now organises the full annual programme of events already described.

1000km and Spa 1000km. A total of ninety-two races were entered altogether and seventy-one finished, yielding twenty-four overall wins, fifteen second places and twenty-seven class wins. Many well-known drivers were involved, including Stirling Moss, Jackie Stewart, Graham Hill, John Surtees, Jo Bonnier, Lorenzo Bandini, Ludovico Scarfiotti, Michael Parkes, Lucien Bianchi and Richard Attwood.

These efforts bore fruit, the business expanded and in 1965 it was moved to new and separate premises at Wellesley Road, Chiswick. Two years later the company moved again, to the Tower Garage on the Egham by-pass. By that time Shaun Bealey, a close friend of Colonel Hoare, had acquired a forty per cent holding in the company, and became a full-time member of its staff.

The introduction of the Dino in 1970 enforced a further and rapid expansion of the business. In 1972 a dealer network was established for the first time. Six Dino dealers were appointed and these formed the foundation of the present British dealer network involving eleven distributors and five dealers. In 1973, 500 cars were sold, and in January 1974 a new purpose-built centre, housing workshops and offices, was opened. It is located on the Thorpe Industrial Estate

The poise and elegance of the Dino 246 is such that the car will never become dated in appearance. It is a true classic.

not far from Egham, the Tower Garage site being retained and used for retail sales.

In the same year the company became the concessionaire for South East Asia, Australia, New Zealand and Japan, setting up Maranello Concessionaires (Australia) Pty Ltd based in Sydney to help conduct this business, as well as Maranello Concessionaires (Orient) Ltd in Hong Kong which is operated by Coopers & Lybrand.

Since then the company has taken over the supply of spare parts for both old and new Ferraris to every country in the world except Italy. Early in 1988 the Colonel and Shaun Bealey sold the business and its overseas subsidiaries to the Tozer, Kemsley and Millbourn Group. Sadly, Colonel Hoare died in September 1989.

There are, however, no plans for change other than steady improvements in efficiency. For Dino owners one of the most important facilities run by Maranello Concessionaires is the Marpart service, which, as already mentioned, includes a large stock of new, reconditioned or remanufactured spares for the 206GT, 246GT and 246GTS. In addition to providing full servicing and repair facilities, the Thorpe centre also houses workshops in which Ferraris are repaired, restored or rebuilt to the highest standards.

Appendix A

Ferrari Clubs of the World

Australian Ferrari Register
Geoff Petherbridge
PO Box 1072
Danenong
Victoria 3175
Australia

Ferrari Owner's Club
35 Market Place
Snettisham
King's Lynn
Norfolk PE31 7LR

Club Ferrari France
Christian Philippsen
109 Rue Aristide Briand
92300 Levallois-Perret
France

Ferrari Club Japan
T. Kirikae
c/o Racing Service Dino
8–8 Ohmachi
Tsuchiura 300
Japan

Club Ferrari NZ
Maurice Paton
16 Toledo Place
Christchurch 8
New Zealand

Ferrari Club Duetshland e.V
Sekretariat Autexpo GmbH
Holderlinstrasse 6
D – 7024 Filderstadt 4
West Germany

Club Ferrari Espana
M. de Miguel Mornet
c/o IRESA Poligono
    Industrial El Segre
Lerida
Spain

Ferrari Club Suisse
Jacques Weber
210 Route de Meyrin
CH-1217 Meyrin/GE
Switzerland

Ferrari Dino Owners' Club
Joachim Alpers
Bruggacherstrasse 12
CH-8617 Monchaltorf
Switzerland

Ferrari Club of America
Karl Dedolph
200 Webber Hills Road
Wayzata
Minnesota 55391
USA

Ferrari Club Belgio
Xavier Van Nuffel
Garage Francorchamps
Rue du Colonel Bourg 107b
1140 Bruxelles
Belgium

Prancing Horse Register
Ray Jenkins
30 Temple Grove
Bakers Lane
West Hanningfield
Chelmsford
Essex CM2 8LQ
England

Ferrari Club Valenza
Sergio Cassano
Via S. Salvatore 21
15048 Valenza (AL)
Italy

Ferrari Club Nederland
N.P.H. Koel
Nievwe Bussummerweg 148
NL–1272 CL
Huizen
Nederland

Southern Equatorial Ferrari
Automobili Club
Giorgio E. Cavalieri
PO Box 7198
Johannesburg 2000
Republic of South Africa

Ferraristi Svezia
Rein Tomson
Tvarskedet 26
S–415 06 Gothenburg
Sweden

Bugatti/Ferrari Owners' Club
Miss Maria Stucheli
Schwalbenstrasse 32C
9202 Gossau
Switzerland

Ferrari Owners' Club (USA)
Pat Benz
1708 Seabright
Long Beach
California 90813
USA

Club Cavallino
Michael Roland
25 Avenue Thery
92420 Vaucresson
France

Club Ferrari Grand-Duche
du Luxembourg
John Wengler
23 rue du Barrage
L-6582 Rosport
Luxembourg

Dino Club Japan
Michitake Isobe
1-5-7 Fujizuka
Kohoku-Ku
Yokohama 222
Japan

Ferrari Club Italia
Renato Carrera
Via dell' Abetone 4
41053 Maranello (MO)
Italy

Ferrari Owners' Club of
Hong Kong
Rory Nicholas
c/o Elders GM (HK) Ltd
18th Floor
Hong Kong Club Building
Chater Road, Hong Kong

Association Collection Ferrari Mas du Clos:
President – Pierre Bardinon
Historian – Claude Vialard

Appendix B

Ferrari Sales & Service Organisations

		Telephone
SURREY	**FERRARI UK (MARANELLO CONCESSIONAIRES LTD)** Thorpe Industrial Estate Thorpe Egham Surrey TW20 8RJ	01784-436222
	Maranello Sales Ltd Egham-By-Pass Egham Surrey TW20 0AX	01784-436431
LONDON	**H.R. Owen** 49/51 Cheval Place London SW7 1EW	0171-225-2007
ESSEX	**Lancaster Garages (Colchester Ltd)** Auto Way Ipswich Road Colchester CO4 4HA	01206-855500
BIRMINGHAM	**Evans Halshaw** Monaco House Bristol Street Birmingham B5 7AU	0121-666-6999
DORSET	**Nigel Mansell Sports Cars Ltd** Salisbury Road Blandford DT11 8UB	01258-451211

		Telephone
NORTHERN IRELAND	**Charles Hurst Ltd** 62 Boucher Road Balmoral Belfast BT12 6LR	01232-381721
YORKSHIRE	**JCT600 Ltd** Tordoff House Sticker Lane Bradford BD4 8QG	01274-779600
TYNE AND WEAR	**Reg Vardy plc** The Car Centre Stoneygate Houghton-le-Spring Tyne and Wear DH4 4NJ	0191-512-0101

		Telephone
LEICESTERSHIRE	**Graypaul** The Coneries Nottingham Road Loughborough LE11 1DZ	01509-232233
SCOTLAND	**Glenvarigill Company Ltd** 300 Colinton Road Edinburgh EH13 0LE	0131-441-1111
	Glenvarigill Company Ltd Maxwell Avenue Bearsden Glasgow G61 2NU	0141-943-1155

		Telephone
CHESHIRE	**Stratstone of Wilmslow** Altrincham Road Wilmslow Cheshire SK9 5NL	01625-522222
GLOUCESTERSHIRE	**Mortimer Houghton Turner Ltd** Midwinter Road Northleach Gloucestershire GL54 3JD	01451-861042 (Sales) 01451-861051 (Service)
CHANNEL ISLANDS	**Melbourne Garage Limited** Routes des Issues St John Jersey CI	01534-862709

Appendix C

Independent Repairers and Restorers

Colin Clark Engineering
247 Acton Lane
London NW10 7NR   0181-961-9392

Kent High Performance Cars
Units 1 & 2
Target Business Centre
Bircholt Road
Parkwood
Maidstone
Kent ME15 9YY   01622-663308

Moto Technique
141 Molesey Avenue
West Molesey
Surrey KT8 0RQ   0181-941-3510

Appendix D

Dino Paintwork and Leather Colours

Paint Colours

Bianco Polo Park
Avorio Safari
Giallo
Nuovo Giallo Fly
Giallo Senape
Verde Germoglio
Verde Scuro 'Dino'
Azzurro Cielo
Azzurro 'Dino'
Bleu Scuro 'Dino'
Rosso 'Dino'
Rosso Chiaro
Rosso Bordeaux
Rosso
Prugna

Nero
Argento Auteuil Metallizzato
Oro Chiaro Metallizzato
Grigio Ferro Metallizzato
Marrone 'Dino' Metallizzato
Nocciola Metallizzato
Celeste Metallizzato
Azzurro Metallizzato
Bleu Chiaro Metallizzato
Blu 'Dino' Metallizzato
Bleu Sera Metallizzato
Verde Medio Metallizzato
Verde Pino Metallizzato
Rosso Rubino Metallizzato
Rosso Cordoba Metallizzato
Viola 'Dino' Metallizzato

Connolly leather was available as follows:

Beige VM 3218
Sabbia VM 3234
Tabacco VM 846
Rosso VM 3171

Nuvola VM 3015
Blu VM 3282
Testa di Moro VM890
Nero VM 8500

Index